Gospels
for the 21st Century

by David Hulme

Vision Media Publishing
Pasadena, California
2010

PUBLISHED BY VISION MEDIA PUBLISHING
P.O. Box 90607
Pasadena, California 91109-0607

Vision Collections are compiled and revised from material
previously published in serial form in the quarterly journal *Vision*
(www.vision.org).

Unless otherwise noted, all scripture references are from the
HOLY BIBLE, NEW INTERNATIONAL VERSION® (© 1973, 1978,
1984 by International Bible Society). Used by permission of
Zondervan Publishing House.

Designed by CDT Design
www.cdt-design.co.uk
Illustrations by Paddy Malloy
www.paddymalloy.com
Printed and bound in the United States of America
by The Castle Press
www.castlepress.com
ISBN 978-0-9822828-0-9

Contents

Foreword

In my many years of detailed research and study about the life of Jesus, I have watched most of the movies depicting His story yet found none of them wholly true to the biblical account. In reviewing books and art with His life as the subject, even from authors and artists who proclaim to believe in His Messiahship, I've had the same experience. How can that be? Jesus is arguably the most well-known and influential person in human history, and after 2,000 years, writers are still producing related works at a rate of hundreds of books each year.

The problem of inaccuracy seems to lie in how the New Testament record is approached. An experience with a major TV network might illuminate the point. I submitted a proposal for a 13-hour series on the New Testament that met with much interest and led to an initial contract. But then the vice president asked me if I could take a more doubtful approach. I explained that I wanted to take the unconventional stance of accepting the biblical record as factual and write the script accordingly. Since, to the best of my knowledge, no TV documentary series had ever taken such a path, this would provide the unique angle considered so important by television executives. I tried to convince him that this view would be refreshing for his audience. A few weeks later, having met with the script editor assigned to the project (who also pressed for a different treatment), I received a note from the vice president expressing regret that the project was being abandoned. Despite his best intentions and personal interest, he could not get his staff to agree with the approach. Doubt triumphed.

This book is the result of taking the New Testament at its word, reading it carefully for what it actually says. For almost 40 years I have found it revealing and liberating to do so, and along the way I have had to correct my own preconceived ideas. If so many can get the simple facts about the life of history's most famous person wrong, what might they do with His teachings and the practices of His earliest students? Regardless of whether you are a believer in Jesus as the Messiah or just interested in learning more about His life and teaching, I think what follows will surprise you and open the door to a more accurate and, I hope, a more enlightened reading.

David Hulme

March 2010

Gospels
for the 21ˢᵗ Century

Introduction

"We have to admit that there is an immeasurable distance between all that we read in the Bible and the practice of the Church and of Christians."

Jacques Ellul

What was it about Jesus Christ that attracted great crowds to listen to Him? Was it the miracles, the parables in everyday language, or the force of His moral teaching? Was it the perceived possibility of the overthrow of Roman rule, or His searing critique of religious corruption? Was it all, some or none of these reasons?

And why, ultimately, did the religious leadership of the day determine to end the work of the man from Galilee?

Answering these questions takes us on a fascinating journey that will probably change your perceptions of Jesus and His original followers.

As we begin, let's get our geographic bearings. Jesus grew up in Galilee, a territory to the north of Judea. It was located at the intersection of trade routes linking the eastern Mediterranean Sea coast with Damascus in Syria and the lands beyond. Its name in the Aramaic language of Jesus' time was *Galil hagoim*—Galilee of the strangers—because along its network of roads passed all manner of peoples. These were the surroundings of Jesus' youth, the places where His father, Joseph, worked as a carpenter.

Near Nazareth was the regional capital city of Sepphoris. Among its ruins today are the remains of a much later fort built around 1260 by the Crusaders. It stands at the top of a hill that dominates the countryside—a now-silent reminder that in the centuries after the death of Jesus of Nazareth, other strangers continued to crisscross Galilee's productive landscape. The Crusaders were drawn not by trade but by religious fervor—Christians seeking to win back their lost holy places from the followers of Muhammad.

What would the man from Nazareth have made of all the bloodshed they committed in His name? Did His message of a coming peaceful kingdom have anything to do with a vicious struggle over holy places? We could ask the same questions today. Religious conflicts have not gone away, and the holy places are still a bone of contention. Surely the principles underlying the faith He exemplified cry out against such strife.

Disappointed Visitors

American author Mark Twain expressed similar thoughts back in 1869. He visited Bethlehem, the place of Christ's birth, and later wrote, "The priests and the members of the Greek and Latin churches cannot come by the same corridor to kneel in the sacred birthplace of the Redeemer, but are compelled to approach and retire by different avenues, lest they quarrel and fight on this holiest ground on earth."[1] It seems that even those who venerate the places Christ may have been, fight among themselves over those locations.

Twain was disappointed by his dusty three-month horseback journey through Syria and Palestine—especially by the many holy sites. He complained that they were often tawdry and commercialized.

Yet in Galilee he found some serenity. One night, sitting outside his tent on the shores of the Sea of Galilee, he marveled at the region's history and associations. "In the starlight," he wrote, "Galilee has no boundaries but the broad compass of the heavens, and is a theater meet for great events; meet for the birth of a religion able to save the world; and meet for the stately Figure appointed to stand upon its stage and proclaim its high decrees."[2]

---

1   *The Innocents Abroad*, Signet Classic, New York (1980), pp. 449–450.
2   Ibid., p. 385.

In the early 1940s, a young British aircraft engineer stationed in Egypt also visited the Holy Land. When he saw the various holy places, he felt a little as Mark Twain had. He was certainly discouraged by the tasteless "sacred" grottos with their trappings of religiosity. He even asked himself whether some of the celebrated Christian sites were really connected with the life and times of the humble man from Nazareth. That young Royal Air Force volunteer was my father. His fascination with the land—and the implications for Western civilization of what happened there—has become my own.

The Earliest Followers

It is common knowledge that Western civilization has its roots in the Greek and Roman worlds. We can see it in our legal systems, our communications, commerce and science, our forms of government, as well as our art and literature. But overlaying that foundation is another powerful influence—the value system found in the Bible, the familiar Book of books. Its principles have guided monarchs, statesmen and ordinary people through the ages.

When Alfred the Great, for example, set down his code of law for the English peoples, he attached a paraphrased translation of the Ten Commandments and abridged passages from a couple of chapters in the book of Exodus—the ones that spell out practical applications of the Ten Commandments. Centuries later on the American continent, the founding fathers of the United States formulated their constitution, guided by that same enduring biblical heritage. So a central part of our Western cultural foundation can be traced to a narrow land at the crossroads of the ancient world.

What did the earliest followers of Jesus have to tell their world? Have Jesus' teachings enjoyed accurate transmission across the years? How much of the original faith still exists? Is the Christian religion we know today in part accumulated misconception?

A hundred and fifty years ago, Danish philosopher Søren Kierkegaard wrote that millions of people through the centuries have "sought little by little to cheat God out of Christianity."[3] It's a shocking assertion. More recently, the French writer Jacques Ellul said, "We have to admit that there is an immeasurable distance between all that we read in the Bible and the practice of the Church and of Christians."[4] If these assertions are correct—if, as Kierkegaard also said, "the Christianity of the New Testament simply does not exist"[5]—then perhaps it's time to go back and rediscover the authentic faith. Our story begins on a Sabbath day in Galilee.

---

3   *Attack Upon "Christendom,"* translated by Walter Lowrie,
     Princeton University Press (1944, 1968), p. 33.
4   *The Subversion of Christianity,* Wm. B. Eerdmans Publishing Company,
     Grand Rapids, Michigan (1986), p. 7.
5   *Attack Upon "Christendom,"* p. 32.

Chapter One

Humble Beginnings

"Jesus . . . did not count equality with God a thing to be grasped, but made himself nothing, taking the form of a servant, being born in the likeness of men."

"The Spirit of the Lord is on me, because he has anointed me to preach good news to the poor. He has sent me to proclaim freedom for the prisoners and recovery of sight for the blind, to release the oppressed, to proclaim the year of the Lord's favor" (Luke 4:18–19, New International Version throughout unless otherwise noted). With these words from the scroll of the prophet Isaiah, Jesus announced His mission in the synagogue of His hometown of Nazareth in the late 20s C.E.

The Gospel writer Luke tells us that at first the townspeople were impressed by the words that came from His lips. "Isn't this Joseph's son?" they asked. But before long, Jesus' teaching angered them, especially when He began to explain that "no prophet is accepted in his hometown." He reminded His listeners of ancient Israel's rejection of its prophets—men of God—who came with unpopular messages. They warned their societies of the need to radically change behavior and live according to God's laws. When Jesus made such pointed statements, His audience was infuriated perhaps as much as their Old Testament forebears had been.

The result of His speech in Nazareth was that the audience took Him to a cliff overlooking the town. They intended to throw Him over the edge and kill Him. And don't people think the same way today? The notion of killing the messenger when we do not like the message is familiar. On this occasion, although it was a close call, Jesus survived. Luke's account simply tells us that Jesus "walked right through the crowd and went on his way."

This early incident in Jesus' ministry reflects the tension He often generated. On the one hand, gracious speech; on the other, uncompromising moral logic that cornered His listeners.

From Conception to Misconception

Jesus' hometown of Nazareth was a very small place at that time. But the village was not His birthplace, of course. That distinction is reserved for Bethlehem, about 90 miles to the south in ancient Judah. It was there that Jesus' parents, Joseph and Mary, had their roots.

Every year at the Christmas season, the town of Bethlehem is filled with pilgrims acknowledging what they believe was the time and place of their Savior's birth. But does the traditional Christmas story reflect what the Bible says? You might be surprised.

Two thousand years ago, the Mediterranean basin was a Roman-dominated world. Just before Jesus was born, the emperor Caesar Augustus (27 B.C.E.–14 C.E.) issued a decree calling for a census. Joseph and Mary had to go to their ancestral home, Bethlehem, to register. When exactly was this? Though the Bible is not as specific as we might like, we are given several clues. One is that King Herod, who searched for the infant Jesus, died in 4 B.C.E.

Luke gives us another indication. He writes about the census: "This was the first registration when Quirinius was governor of Syria. And all went to be registered, each to his own town" (Luke 2:2–3, English Standard Version). This translation suggests that more than one census occurred under Quirinius's supervision. We know from Roman records that he was governor from 6 to 7 C.E. But this is too late for Jesus' birth. While some scholars argue that there were two officials named Quirinius, it could be that the same man conducted two registrations, the first around 6 to 4 B.C.E. Since we're told Jesus was born during Quirinius's first census, this is one way that the birth can be dated approximately. An alternate translation reads, "This was the census that took place *before* Quirinius was governor of Syria" (emphasis added); i.e., he was in charge of the census, but not yet governor. This would also confirm a date prior to 6 C.E.

Note that this book uses the designations "C.E." (common era) and "B.C.E." (before the common era) instead of "A.D" (*anno Domini,* "in the year of our Lord") and "B.C." (before Christ). The latter terms are in fact inaccurate. But where did the idea come from to divide time into "B.C." and "A.D."? Surprisingly, it wasn't until 526 C.E. that a Scythian monk, Dionysius Exiguus, living in Rome, created this method of dating. And it was not until a thousand years later that "B.C." came into use. Gradually the now common misconception took hold that Christ was born at the division of the years between B.C. and A.D. But the few historical benchmarks given in the New Testament give no support to such a conclusion.

Another misconception concerns not the year but the day of Christ's birth. It is now known that December 25 could not have been the date. More likely, Jesus was born in the early autumn. We can establish this general period from specific details in the Gospel of Luke.

The temple at Jerusalem had well-defined priestly serving cycles. John the Baptist's father was one of those serving in Jerusalem from time to time. He was designated to serve in the course or cycle named after Abijah, head of one of the priestly families in the days of King David. The timing of the Abijah course was around July-August. The Gospel of Luke tells us that John the Baptist was conceived just after one such visit to Jerusalem. And we also know from Luke that John was about six months older than Jesus. We can establish by simple arithmetic that John was born in the springtime in Palestine, and that Jesus was therefore born in the autumn.

Significant Humility

Joseph and Mary must have had a difficult time getting to Bethlehem. The journey would have taken three to five days. To get to their destination, they probably took the usual route: from Nazareth down the Jordan Valley to Jericho. From there they would climb almost 4,000 feet to Jerusalem and Bethlehem.

As the young parents-to-be traveled along trade routes and regional roads, they no doubt spoke of all that had brought them to this moment. Mary was pregnant, though still a virgin. How could that be? Luke tells of an angelic vision revealing to Mary that her child would be the Messiah, the One long awaited by the Jewish people.

Joseph's first thought had been to break their betrothal agreement in a form of private divorce, avoiding the embarrassment Mary would experience otherwise. For more information, we have to turn to another of the four Gospel writers, Matthew. He tells us that Joseph "was a righteous man and did not want to expose [Mary] to public disgrace" (Matthew 1:19). Joseph soon understood from an inspired dream that he should continue with the marriage. The child, he now knew, was conceived by God's intervention.

It was all very difficult to understand, but Joseph's strong belief in the divine message motivated him to complete the marriage agreement. After all, the Hebrew Scriptures had foretold that a virgin would conceive a son named Emmanuel, meaning "God with us." Joseph and Mary were sufficiently convinced by their unusual experiences to believe that God was involved.

Let's now look at some of the circumstances and the myths surrounding the birth of Christ.

When Joseph and Mary arrived in Bethlehem—birthplace of Israel's most famous king, David—they found that the Roman census had brought many people home. That meant rooms were scarce. Luke says "there was no room for them in the inn."

As it turned out, the circumstances gave Jesus' birth a significant humility. This King of kings and Lord of lords would be born in a stable, which, according to numerous scholars and commentators, could have been inside a cave in one of Bethlehem's hillsides.

The birth of Mary's firstborn son attracted the immediate attention of humble shepherds who had also heard and seen angelic beings—this time announcing the extraordinary birth. In the fields near Bethlehem, the shepherds were watching over their flocks. This suggests that Jesus' birth was not in the middle of winter, when shepherds and flocks do not stay out at night. It does snow in Bethlehem in winter.

The angel told the shepherds that the *Christos*, or Messiah, the long-awaited Savior of mankind, had come. The sign the shepherds should look for was a baby lying in an animals' feeding trough—a manger. In or near the village they found the child and His parents exactly as mentioned. Overwhelmed by the accuracy of the angelic message, the shepherds became the first humans to announce Jesus' birth.

It was a world looking for a messiah; in fact, messianic expectation was commonplace. Some of the Jews wanted liberation from their Roman oppressors—*their* messiah would be a political leader. Others wanted deliverance from disease and every human woe.

And it was not only in Israel that a savior was anticipated.

Long-Predicted Holy One

About 40 years before the birth of Jesus, the Latin poet Virgil wrote that "a God-like child shall be born. . . . Come quickly to receive your power," he said, "for all the world awaits you. Oh that I may live to see so noble a subject for my verse."

The prediction of such a child was an ancient tradition, even in China, where in the early 500s B.C.E. the philosopher Confucius wrote that "the Holy One must be sought in the West."

As a result, some histories mention that about 70 years after Jesus' birth the Chinese emperor Mimti, under the influence of this expectation, sent messengers westward into India to inquire after the long-predicted "Holy One" of Confucius.

A ruler in India had also understood that the birth of this unusual child was to occur. In about 1 C.E., he sent emissaries to Palestine to know whether the predicted royal child had actually made his appearance.

But a child born in a stable did not seem to fit the messianic expectation at all. And yet those mysterious visitors, the Magi or wise men referred to in Matthew's Gospel account, had a different opinion.

Matthew tells us that some time after Jesus' birth, "wise men" came from the east in pursuit of a star. They inquired about "the one who has been born king of the Jews." In the details of this story we begin to unravel more of the misconceptions about Jesus and the belief and practice of the early Church.

Notice that the New Testament record says nothing about how many wise men came. Nonbiblical tradition tells us there were *three*, even three *kings*. But apparently the "three kings" theme did not become popular until the Middle Ages. The New Testament record is silent about the Magi as three kings.

Tradition further misleads us, saying the Magi visited Jesus at His manger. Even the second-century church historian Justin Martyr was at variance with the biblical account with respect to the Magi's visit. He wrote: "When the Child was born in Bethlehem, since Joseph could not find lodging in that village, he took up his quarters in a certain cave near the village; and while they were there Mary brought forth the Christ and placed him in a manger, and here the Magi who came from Arabia found him."

Yet notice the words of Matthew's Gospel about the wise men: "The star they had seen in the east went ahead of them until it stopped over the place where the child was. When they saw the star, they were overjoyed. On coming to the house, they saw the child with his mother Mary . . ." (Matthew 2:9–11). These visitors came to see a *child* in a *house*, not a newborn in a stable.

The King Escapes

As astrologers or philosophers, the Magi were likely aware of the messianic expectations of the age. When their observations of the night sky recorded an unusual star, they journeyed west following its uncharacteristic movements.

Their travels took them first to Jerusalem, since the one they were seeking was to be a new king of the Jews. Because of their questions, they gained an audience with the elderly and paranoid Herod in his palace. Despite his great public works and the loyalty they engendered, Herod was clearly disturbed by the threat of a rival king. Calling for the Jewish religious leaders, he asked where the Messiah was to be born. "'In Bethlehem in Judea,' they replied, 'for this is what the prophet has written . . .'" (verse 5).

The deceitful Herod then sent the Magi to find the child and return with a report "so that I too may go and worship him." However, the men were warned in a dream to avoid Herod, and they returned home by another way. Herod's anger knew no bounds when he discovered the Magi's surreptitious departure. Using the information they had given him about the star's first appearance, he ordered the brutal killing of all boys aged two and younger.

Another message came to Joseph and Mary: this time they were told to flee from Herod's wrath. They immediately took their young son and escaped to Egypt by night. Nothing is known of their refuge in Egypt—neither place nor exact length of time—except that they returned to Nazareth after Herod's death.

A Childhood Experience

During the subsequent years in Galilee, Jesus apparently grew in wisdom and stature, and in favor with God and man. Luke tells us that He developed well under His parents' care.

The only recorded account of His boyhood years was an unusual event in Jerusalem. His well-known interaction with the teachers of the law in the courts of the temple is recounted in Luke 2:41–47. At the Passover season, when He was 12 years old, Jesus became separated from His parents. For three days, unbeknown to Mary and Joseph, He held His scholarly listeners spellbound with questions of great depth and understanding.

Naturally His parents expressed anxiety and concern for their missing son and no doubt some irritation at His apparent lack of concern for them. But this was a defining moment and one Mary would later ponder. When His parents eventually found Him, Jesus answered them with the questions "Why were you searching for me?" and "Didn't you know I had to be in my Father's house?" (verse 49) or "about My Father's business?" (New King James Version). But at this point his parents did not understand, though His mother "treasured all these things in her heart."

Where did Jesus spend the remainder of His youth and early adult life? It can only be a matter of intelligent guesswork since none of the Gospel writers mentions anything about Jesus between the ages of 12 and about 30.

Laying the Foundation

Luke records in verse 51 that Jesus returned to Nazareth from Jerusalem and was obedient to His parents. That relationship no doubt allowed Jesus to learn from Joseph the craft of a carpenter.

The carpenter's role could have taken Joseph around the environs of Nazareth. A discovery near Jesus' boyhood home allows us to speculate reasonably about His youth and what He might have learned as a carpenter's apprentice.

Though the Gospel accounts don't mention Sepphoris, archaeological excavations indicate that it was an important city four miles north of Nazareth. It served as the provincial capital of Galilee during Jesus' time. In this case, what the Gospels do *not* mention forms the basis of an informed opinion. We know that Jesus grew up with a carpenter for a father, that He was obedient to His parents' wishes, and that Nazareth was His family home. We also know that after Herod the Great's death, Herod's kingdom was divided among his three sons, Archelaus, Antipas and Philip.

Herod Antipas ruled Galilee and began an extensive rebuilding program in the gateway city of Sepphoris. The construction continued throughout Jesus' youth at Nazareth. It is therefore possible that Joseph and Jesus worked on the project. Carpenters in those days were also stonemasons, and the scale and grandeur of Sepphoris would have kept local artisans busy for years.

Herod Antipas had been educated with his brother Archelaus in Rome. His experiences immediately before his return to Palestine were entirely in a Roman imperial context. It is no surprise, then, that Sepphoris was a city built in the Roman architectural style, with an amphitheater, baths, government buildings and so on.

If Jesus did experience urban life at Sepphoris, it would have taught significant lessons about trade and business, and about politics and human government. What is often missed in explaining the Gospels is the political atmosphere of Christ's time.

Also overlooked is the political milieu of John the Baptist's ministry.

An Unusual Message

John the Baptist was almost as controversial as Jesus Himself. Giving the historical and geographical context,

Luke says: "In the fifteenth year of the reign of Tiberius Caesar—when Pontius Pilate was governor of Judea, Herod tetrarch of Galilee, his brother Philip tetrarch of Iturea and Traconitis, and Lysanias tetrarch of Abilene— during the high priesthood of Annas and Caiaphas, the word of God came to John son of Zechariah in the desert" (Luke 3:1–2).

The result was that John the Baptist began preaching that repentance of sin before God was essential and that baptism by immersion in the River Jordan would begin the renewal process.

It was an unusual message at the time, in that baptism was not a common ritual. Certainly the prophets of old had spoken of repentance and forgiveness of sin. The Jewish people were also familiar with ritual purification baths, but washing sins away was new.

The Baptist's life had paralleled Jesus' own in several ways. John and Jesus were kinsmen—their mothers were related. Both John's mother, Elizabeth, and Mary had conceived miraculously within a few months of each other. Elizabeth knew that her pregnancy was as much a remarkable sign of divine intervention as Mary's. Elizabeth had been unable to bear children until her old age. When the two met in the early days of Mary's pregnancy, Elizabeth's child had moved suddenly in the womb, and Elizabeth took this as a meaningful sign.

Qumran Connection

It is likely that John's older parents died before he became an adult. It is also possible that as an orphan he was brought up in a religious desert community.

Such a community might have existed at the well-known Qumran, overlooking the Dead Sea. The inhabitants were possibly Essenes, a reclusive and strict sect of the Jews. If they lived in the desolate surroundings on the edge of the Judean wilderness, they certainly lived an ascetic life. The Essenes were awaiting a messiah who would deliver them politically—a warrior king. Then, they believed, a priestly messiah would come to Jerusalem to purify temple worship as well as the sacrifices.

John the Baptist had little in common with such views, but as we've noted, he did practice the ritual of baptism by immersion. At the ruins of Qumran, there are what look like ritual baths or *miqva'ot*, where immersions could have taken place as acts of purification.

Apparently the members of the Qumran community spent a lot of their time copying out the Hebrew Scriptures and writing their own commentaries on them. Perhaps this explains why many inkwells have been found there—certainly an unusual item to discover in large quantities.

Of course, the caves in the area are most famous for the 1947 discovery of the Dead Sea Scrolls. In three of the caves, fragments of a manuscript known as the Cairo Damascus Document were found. They mention a diet including locusts, something the Gospels tell us John ate. This was not necessarily unusual, since the Jews considered locusts fit for food.

A further indication of John the Baptist's possible Qumran connection is the fact that, like John, the community used a verse from Isaiah to describe their purpose. That verse reads, in part, "A voice of one calling: 'In the desert prepare the way for the LORD'" (Isaiah 40:3).

It must be said, however, that John and the Qumran community used the verse to different ends. If John did have anything to do with the community, he moved away from them once his public work began in the 15th year of Tiberius Caesar.

The Hebrew Scriptures are often used by the Gospel writers as supporting evidence for the subject at hand—for example, the mission of John the Baptist. This shouldn't surprise us: the only "Bible" the Gospel writers had was what we call today the Old Testament.

Prescription for Today

John was a fiery preacher. He was one to straighten things out without fear of man. When the people from Judea and Jerusalem went to the Jordan River to hear John, he didn't spare his words. Identifying certain religious leaders among his audience, he characterized them publicly as a "brood of vipers." He warned them that divine retribution will come to the unrepentant, that complacency is a trap, and that a show of religiosity is not enough. A change of heart is what God wants to see.

In this respect, John's mission was not unlike that of the Old Testament prophets. His prescription for behavioral change was the same. When asked for advice on how to practice righteous living, John would reply with specifics, such as "The man with two tunics should share with him who has none, and the one who has food should do the same."

The much-hated tax collectors also sought his advice. To them he said: "Don't collect any more than you are required to."

Then the soldiers came: "'And what should we do?' He replied, 'Don't extort money and don't accuse people falsely—be content with your pay'" (Luke 3:11–14).

Share your goods, don't take more than you should, don't steal or accuse others falsely, and be content with your pay—these sound like prescriptions for today.

And of course, they are, because John's expression of right values, based in the Hebrew Scriptures, was timeless. That's an important aspect of original New Testament teaching—its timelessness. It's something we will continue to note throughout this book.

More Powerful Than John

The kind of discussion John had with his audiences led some to wonder whether he was the anticipated Messiah. Could he be the *Christos* to come?

John's answer to this was emphatic and at the same time puzzling. He said: "I baptize you with water. But one more powerful than I will come, the thongs of whose sandals I am not worthy to untie. He will baptize you with the Holy Spirit and with fire. His winnowing fork is in his hand, to clear his threshing floor and to gather the wheat into his barn, but he will burn up the chaff with unquenchable fire" (verses 16–17).

Whoever he was speaking of had not yet been publicly revealed. But soon Jesus came from Galilee. John reacted to Jesus' request for baptism by declaring, "I need to be baptized by you, and do you come to me?" (Matthew 3:14).

Jesus' reply was that it was necessary to complete the ceremony so that His own life story would set the course for all human beings. That is, everyone at some point must accept or reject purification before God. If Jesus was to serve as a living example for all, then this part of the human experience could not be excluded.

Exactly where along the Jordan John baptized Jesus is unknown, but what happened is explained in all four Gospels. As Jesus came up out of the river, what appeared to be a dove—a symbol of the Holy Spirit—descended on Him. And a voice was heard, saying, "This is my Son, whom I love; with him I am well pleased" (Matthew 3:13–17; Mark 1:9–11; Luke 3:21–22; John 1:32).

After this simple but profound ceremony, Jesus, at the age of about 30, began His public work.

The Tempter's Trap

Jesus' immediate challenge concerned the use of His considerable powers for His own purposes. Immediately after His baptism, He was led by the Spirit into the wilderness to meet an opponent from the spirit world: after having fasted 40 days, Jesus encountered Satan the devil.

Matthew describes His opponent's first line of attack: "If you are the Son of God, tell these stones to become bread" (Matthew 4:3).

The craving for food was no doubt intense. The knowledge of His own power to miraculously change the circumstances was also present with Jesus. Was this an opportunity to use it for personal benefit?

Christ's reply was simply, "Man does not live on bread alone, but on every word that comes from the mouth of God."

The tempter then made two more appeals. Why not throw yourself from the highest point on the temple's walls?

Surely God will save you. After all, you could prove who you are by taking what would be a suicidal leap, because the Scriptures promise your protection: "'He will command his angels concerning you, and they will lift you up in their hands, so that you will not strike your foot against a stone,'" quoted the tempter.

But Jesus knew that testing God's protection would be willful and wrong. His response? "Do not put the Lord your God to the test."

Finally, the devil took Christ to a high mountain and surveyed the kingdoms of the world. "'All this I will give you,' he said, 'if you will bow down and worship me.'"

His offer was seductive in the sense that Jesus knew His destiny was ultimately to have rulership of the world—but only on His Father's terms, not as Satan's slave. His reply was final: "Away from me, Satan! For it is written: 'Worship the Lord your God, and serve him only.'"

This account of the temptation is followed in the Gospel of John by more details about the role of John the Baptist. The religious leaders were obviously perplexed by his ministry and wanted to know who he really was. The Pharisees, having suffered his verbal attacks, sent some of their Sadducee associates from Jerusalem to speak with John.

"Are you the Christ?" they asked.

"No," said John, "nor am I Elijah, nor the Prophet foretold in the Scriptures. I am simply the messenger coming before the Lord" (John 1:19–28, paraphrased).

The next day, John identified Jesus as "the Lamb of God"—the one who was prophesied to come as a sacrificial offering for humanity (verse 29). And the following day he repeated the phrase to two of his disciples, one of whom was

Andrew. Both then became followers of Jesus, along with Andrew's brother, Simon Peter.

First Public Miracle

At this point Jesus went back to His home region of Galilee, and His public ministry began to emerge alongside that of John. Within a few days, Jesus had attracted two more disciples, Philip and Nathanael.

According to John's Gospel, it was now that Jesus' first public miracle occurred. At Cana in Galilee, Jesus, His mother and His disciples were invited to a wedding. During the feast, the supply of wine ran out, and Mary mentioned this to her son. Jesus' reaction suggests that she knew He could provide more wine, but that He preferred not to do so to avoid notoriety.

"Dear woman, why do you involve me?" He asked. "My time has not yet come" (John 2:4).

But His mother told the servants to help Jesus in whatever way He asked. They filled six stone jars with water, which then miraculously became wine—120 to 180 gallons in all. And there can be no mistake: it *was* wine. The New Testament Greek word used is *oinos*—"fermented grape juice."

The steward of the wedding feast was pleasantly surprised. He told the bridegroom, "Everyone brings out the choice wine first and then the cheaper wine after the guests have had too much to drink; but you have saved the best till now." The miracle had the effect of confirming to His disciples that Jesus was from God.

From Cana, on the upper plateau of Galilee, Jesus and His family and disciples traveled down to Capernaum at the northern end of the Sea of Galilee, where He would eventually set up a home. But after a few days there, it was Passover season and time to travel to Jerusalem.

Destroy the Temple?

When Jesus arrived at the temple area, He found the merchants and money changers trading in the outer courts. The money changers were inclined to cheat in their foreign-exchange dealings. Jewish visitors came to Jerusalem from all over the known world and brought with them their currencies. They also had to pay temple tax, which required a certain kind of coin from the ancient city of Tyre. Here again the money changers could easily gouge their customers. No doubt similar price-fixing occurred when animals and birds for commanded sacrifices were bought from the merchants. The law of supply and demand always induces greed when morality is absent.

All of this corruption brought Jesus' condemnation as He drove the traders out of the temple enclosure: "How dare you turn my Father's house into a market!" He said (John 2:16). It was an unprecedented action that caused the religious leaders to ask Jesus for a sign of who He was and by what authority He did such things.

His reply was enigmatic. He said, "Destroy this temple, and I will raise it again in three days."

To the Jewish leaders this sounded like a preposterous and arrogant claim. How could He rebuild in three days something that had taken years to construct? Jesus was speaking, of course, not of the actual temple but of His own physical body, which, once dead, would be resurrected. After His death, His disciples would recall this unusual statement.

Teaching the Teacher

The Passover season also provided for an important private meeting between Jesus and a key religious leader. Jesus' popularity was growing—His public statements and miraculous works were drawing increasing attention. Nicodemus, a prominent man in the religious community, came to Jesus under cover of darkness. He acknowledged that the Pharisees knew that Jesus was a teacher sent from God because of the miracles He was performing. Jesus took the opportunity to explain some truths to this leader that he ought to have known.

He told Nicodemus that the kingdom of God is something that is spiritually discerned and that entry into that kingdom is the destiny of humans who come to have a Spirit-led mind.

It is significant that a religious leader could be as unaware as the unconvinced and unconverted. This speaks to the vital importance of a mind that is truly open to God's Word. Jesus said to Nicodemus, "You are Israel's teacher, and do you not understand these things?" (John 3:10).

Jesus went on to explain that belief in His coming was essential to entry into the kingdom of God. God the Father had given the Son to be a sacrifice for all humanity. People who didn't want to walk in the light would not come to the Son. The light of truth exposes evil intentions and evil acts.

It was exactly that kind of behavior that John the Baptist was combating. John was still at work baptizing in the Jordan valley. A dispute arose between some of his disciples and the Jews about purification, and about Jesus' role in baptizing people. John took the position that his own work would now diminish, as Christ's would expand.

It was a humble recognition that his part was almost done. Shortly John would be thrown into prison as a political prisoner of Herod Antipas. John had been forthright in criticizing the ruler for his marriage to his brother's wife (who, according to first-century Jewish historian Josephus, was also his niece); the openly adulterous and incestuous relationship was well known—and against the law of God (see Leviticus 18:6, 16; 20:21). As a result, John was soon to be silenced.

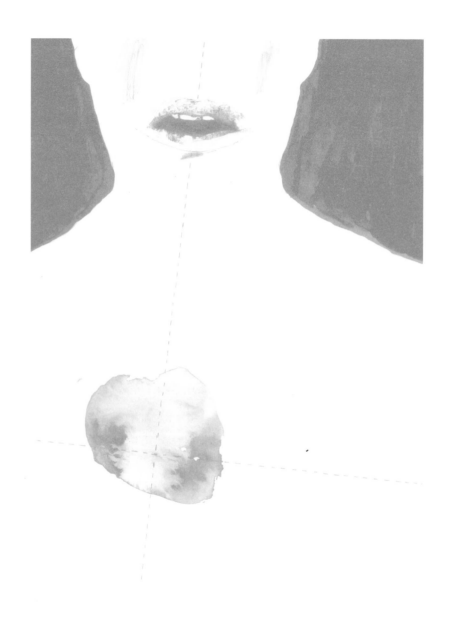

Chapter Two

Understanding the Human Heart

As Jesus' following grew, so grew the need to teach the moral core of discipleship. To that end, Jesus delivered to His disciples what has been termed the greatest moral discourse of all time: the Sermon on the Mount.

Machaerus is an ancient hilltop fortress on the eastern side of the Dead Sea. It may seem an unlikely place to pursue our study of Jesus of Nazareth, especially when there is no evidence that He ever went there. Machaerus was once part of Herod the Great's line of fortified defenses. All that remains today are the outlines of a few rooms. But in the first century, it contained a palace with plastered walls, mosaic floors and an extensive water- and food-supply system.

It also served as the prison for John the Baptist. And this fact provides the connection with Jesus of Nazareth. What happened to John in the fortress played an important part in initiating Jesus' own ministry. John had spoken plainly about Herod Antipas's wickedness. He had also intruded on Herod's personal life with his criticisms, telling the ruler that he had no right to steal the wife of his half brother Philip.

According to Josephus, it was Herod's suspicious mind that led to John's imprisonment. It seems that he also feared John's popularity with the people and thought that the Baptizer might start a rebellion against him.

Living Water

The Gospel writer Mark tells us that when Jesus heard that John's preaching had been silenced, He traveled to Galilee preaching the gospel of the kingdom of God, thus beginning His own three-and-a-half-year ministry (Mark 1:14–15). On the way from Judea He passed through Samaria and stopped at a famous well, named after the patriarch Jacob. A woman came to draw water, and Jesus asked her for a drink (John 4:4–7).

The Jews and the Samaritans were traditional opponents, the Jews looking down on their northern neighbors as a religiously and tribally inferior people. So the woman was puzzled that a Jew would ask water from a Samaritan. It would, after all, make him ritually unclean.

Jesus explained that if she had truly recognized Him she would have asked Him for *living water*. Inviting her to gain some spiritual understanding, Jesus engaged her in a conversation that revealed who He was and His ability to read the human heart.

The woman, it turned out, had had five husbands and was now living with a man who was not her husband. Jesus perceived all of this and shocked the woman by telling her so. This led to her recognition of Jesus' special discernment, and that perhaps He was a prophet (verses 9–19).

Jesus in turn explained to her that the Samaritan religion was in error and that He, in fact, was the Messiah to come. Needless to say, it was an astonishing revelation. For the first time Jesus openly said who He was. Yet He did not tell it to His own people but to a Samaritan woman. This is quite an irony, because she and her townspeople came to recognize Him as "the Savior of the world" (verses 39–42), while at the same time many of His own people did not.

Dawning Light

At this point we will begin to trace Jesus' footsteps around Galilee. We will turn our attention to the heart and core of His ethical and moral teaching—found in some of the most remarkable passages of the New Testament. These are some of the great truths embedded in the Western cultural heritage; yet so often, it seems, we are unfamiliar with their origin or the thought that lies behind these universal truths.

It was in Capernaum, at the northern end of the Sea of Galilee, that Jesus took up residence after the people of

His hometown, Nazareth, rejected His mission. The small fishing village became the base for His work of teaching and healing.

Capernaum's location in Galilee placed it in the land populated in ancient times by the Israelite tribes of Zebulun and Naphtali. The Gospel writer Matthew tells us that Jesus' coming to Capernaum fulfilled an Old Testament promise. Isaiah the prophet had said: "Land of Zebulun and land of Naphtali, the way to the sea, along the Jordan, Galilee of the Gentiles—the people living in darkness have seen a great light; on those living in the land of the shadow of death a light has dawned" (Matthew 4:13–16).

According to Matthew, the light that dawned was Jesus and the truth He would bring to Galilee and the world. Matthew used Isaiah's words to show his Jewish audience scriptural support for Jesus' mission.

But why did Jesus concentrate on Galilee? Why was it the center of His work? Why did He go back to Galilee from Judea once He heard that John the Baptist was in prison?

As we have noted, Galilee was near the main trade route between the Mediterranean and Damascus and the East. It was a stop along the way for the foreigners, or gentiles, who came and went with their exotic cargoes. It is likely that Galilee had an intellectual openness that would permit Jesus' teaching to flourish for a while. And the crossroads environment of Galilee meant that word of Jesus' activities could spread far and wide.

Fishers of Men

During Roman times, the fresh waters of the Sea of Galilee provided for a lucrative fishing trade. It is no surprise, then, that some among Jesus' early followers were partners in the fishing business. Their names are familiar: the brothers Andrew and Simon Peter, and the sons of Zebedee, James and John.

Luke's Gospel tells us that one day Jesus was walking by the Sea of Galilee. Seeing Simon, He asked if He would take Him out a little way in the boat. Offshore, Jesus could speak to the crowds more easily, His voice carrying over the water. Simon had heard Jesus teach before (beginning, as we saw earlier, after his brother Andrew heard John the Baptist proclaim Jesus as "the Lamb of God"), but now he had the chance to listen again in the peace and quiet of the lake's surroundings.

When Jesus finished teaching, He told Simon to go out into deeper water and let down his net for a large catch. We're told that Simon and his men, despite having caught nothing all night, immediately caught so many fish that their boat was in danger of sinking. And not only *their* boat—Simon had to call on James and John to help. They hauled in so many fish that they, too, were endangered (Luke 5:1–7).

What lesson would they draw from this unusual experience? Jesus' message to the fishermen was simple: Don't be afraid; from now on you'll be netting not just fish, but an abundance of men and women for the kingdom of God.

The experience was dramatic enough to become a turning point for those early disciples. They immediately left their occupations and became full-time participants in Jesus' work. It was a decision that would take them all over Roman Palestine and beyond. Their own land was, of course, familiar territory, but what they would learn from Jesus was something entirely new and unfamiliar.

Speaking With Authority

It was apparently Jesus' practice to teach in one synagogue or another on the Sabbath day. In Capernaum, a God-fearing Roman centurion had built a synagogue for the Jews. The man was so well loved that when his servant was taken ill, the Jewish elders summoned Jesus to help him.

The synagogue that most visitors to Galilee are shown when they go to the Holy Land to walk where Jesus walked is of third- or fourth-century construction. But in the foundations are the black basalt footings of an earlier building—perhaps the original synagogue that Jesus knew.

In such simple buildings, Jesus astonished His listeners because He taught with unusual authority. Unlike His contemporaries, He didn't quote others to support His case. He simply showed the scriptural principles from the Law and the Prophets, and detailed the teaching with analogies from everyday life.

In the first-century synagogue, the Jewish rabbis generally taught from a central seated position. If Jesus did the same, He would have had much more contact with the audience than in today's synagogues and churches.

Typically Jesus would have read from the scrolls of Scripture kept at the synagogue and then commented on them. It seems He was an impressive speaker. And it wasn't just the regular worshipers who were amazed by His authority; even those mentally troubled by the spirits shouted out in recognition of Him.

Luke tells us that one day in the Capernaum synagogue there was just such a man. He was afflicted with what today some might call a multiple personality disorder. In this man's case, the spirit of these various personalities suddenly spoke out: "What do you want with us, Jesus of Nazareth? Have you come to destroy us? I know who you are—the Holy One of God!" (Luke 4:31–34).

And what was Jesus' response? Simply to command the spirit to leave so that the man's sanity could quickly return.

It was a startling event. It caused a great stir and spread Jesus' reputation all around the region of Galilee. A man who could tame a troublesome spirit was rare indeed.

More Misconceptions

In Chapter 1, we discovered some common misconceptions about the New Testament story, such as the date of Jesus' birth, which we found was not December 25 or anywhere close.

Now we're about to uncover another myth. For too long, traditional Christianity has had the idea that the disciples, and even Jesus Himself, lived out on the road—that the disciples were mostly homeless, unmarried and poverty-stricken. Yet clearly the New Testament shows that Peter had a home, a wife, and for a time even a fishing business.

The Gospel of Mark describes a visit to Peter's house by Jesus. It says: "As soon as they left the synagogue, they went with James and John to the home of Simon and Andrew. Simon's mother-in-law was in bed with a fever, and they told Jesus about her. So he went to her, took her hand and helped her up. The fever left her and she began to wait on them" (Mark 1:29–31).

By the end of that Sabbath, on Saturday evening, many were at the door begging for Jesus' healing. He helped them, of course, but He also told some of those who had been mentally disturbed not to say who He was—the Christ, or Messiah (Luke 4:40–41). It wasn't time yet to have that title broadcast, or, like John the Baptist, Jesus could be caught up in Herod Antipas's paranoia and silenced. It was Antipas's father, Herod the Great, who'd tried to kill Jesus just after He was born. In the early days of His ministry, Jesus did not need to invite Herod Antipas's opposition.

The next day, before dawn, Jesus went out alone to an isolated place to pray. Here was an opportunity to reappraise the situation. After some time, His disciples came looking for Him. They told Him that the people of Capernaum wanted more of His attention. But Jesus was now convinced He had to move on and teach in other towns and villages (Mark 1:35–39).

And so began His first great tour of the Galilean region.

Widening the Arc of Ministry

Jesus' travels only enhanced His reputation. Matthew says that great crowds traveled from far afield to hear and be healed (Matthew 4:23–25). No longer did they come just from Galilee. There were people from the Decapolis—a region of 10 sophisticated cities of Greek culture southeast of the Sea of Galilee. The southernmost of these cities was Philadelphia, which is today Amman, capital of Jordan. People also came from Perea, on the east bank of the River Jordan, and from Judea and Jerusalem.

On His teaching tour, Jesus continued to heal all kinds of sickness, from epilepsy and paralysis to leprosy and various mental illnesses. But He was still wary of the acclaim His actions would bring. From time to time He would withdraw from the public eye for a while.

All the same, His activities were becoming an irritant to the local religious leadership. They obviously feared Jesus' popularity with their people, and they began to look for every opportunity to criticize.

On one occasion, as Jesus healed a paralyzed man, He said something that astonished His critics. He told the man that his sins were forgiven. The Pharisees and doctors of the law overheard and immediately began to accuse Jesus of blasphemy (Mark 2:1–7).

Perhaps it seems like an overreaction to us. What was blasphemous about what Jesus had said? In claiming to forgive sin, He put Himself on a level with God in the Pharisees' eyes—for only God could forgive sin.

Of course, the message Jesus wanted to send was that He, as the son of man and the Son of God, *had* the power to forgive sin. To emphasize the truth of His statement and its spiritual significance for everyone, Jesus restored the paralytic's ability to walk (verses 8–12).

It was an amazing event. But would we believe it if it happened today? Would we believe in a man who really healed miraculously? It's something to think about in view of the religious confusion that surrounds us today.

As His following grew, so grew the need to teach the moral core of discipleship. To that end, Jesus delivered to His disciples what has been termed the greatest moral discourse of all time: the Sermon on the Mount.

A Richer Vessel

Symptomatic of our contemporary religious uncertainty is the question that a leading newsmagazine asked on its front cover: "Who was Jesus?" The fact that such a question even needs to be asked would indicate that much of Jesus' *teaching* has also likely been misunderstood or forgotten.

Take, for example, what Jesus said to a paralyzed man whom He healed (Matthew 9:2). The issue was *sin*—an unfashionable concept in our time. Have we perhaps reached the point where we find it difficult to say that anyone is really guilty of anything? That sin even exists? After all, society has taught us to make patients out of sinners. People no longer "sin"; they're victims of the past, or of their parents, or of "the system." But Western civilization's foundational teachings say otherwise. The Bible tells us we do sin. And if we feel guilty as a result, that's essentially a good thing. Guilt can be good for us, especially if it leads to changed, healthy behavior through God's forgiveness.

When Jesus simultaneously healed the paralyzed man and forgave his sins, He was signaling not only that sin is a paralyzing force in human life, but also that He was able to relieve the burden of sin and of a guilty conscience. "Come to me, all you who are weary and burdened, and I will give you rest," He said (Matthew 11:28).

It was a message that obviously impressed the Galilean tax collector Matthew Levi. He, too, lived in Capernaum. The town was on the border between two Herodian territories and had a customs post for tax collection. Matthew was at work one day when Jesus came by and asked him to join in His teaching mission. Matthew agreed and soon prepared a meal in his own house to celebrate. He invited several other tax-collector friends (Matthew 9:9–10).

In Jesus' time, tax officials were despised—especially by the religious leaders, who objected to their frequent cheating. As it was, taxes could be as high as 40 percent. To make matters worse, the tax money was used to support the ruling Herodians and their Roman masters.

But Jesus made it clear that mixing with despised people like the cheating tax collectors was not a sin. It was an opportunity to help them make spiritual progress.

True Religion

Here was the great difference between Jesus of Nazareth and His religious contemporaries. He really cared for people, for their problems and their struggles; He understood their lot in life. The religious leaders, it seems, were more interested in maintaining their own power and prestige. They cared little for the people or the real spiritual issues. Their religious observance had become a ball and chain, preventing them from practicing true religion from the heart. It was form, not substance—ritual, not reality.

Jesus illustrated this in three telling parables. And in doing so, He answered yet another complaint from the Pharisees. This time even the disciples of John the Baptist had joined in the criticism. It's possible that while Jesus and His disciples were feasting with Matthew the tax collector and his friends, John's disciples and the Pharisees were deliberately going without food: they were fasting. Perhaps it was one of their self-imposed fast days.

"Why don't your disciples fast like we do?" they asked Jesus (Matthew 9:14, paraphrased). His three-part reply to their critical question (verses 15–17) was somewhat puzzling. First, He said, as long as the bridegroom is present, the wedding guests don't stop feasting. Then He added that people don't sew a patch of new cloth on old material, for fear of making the tear worse. Third, in a now famous phrase, he said that men do not put new wine in old wineskins for fear of losing both. New wine will burst an old wineskin. John's disciples and the Pharisees were left wondering whether they were the old wineskins incapable of taking in the new truth that Jesus had brought.

Concluding His thoughts on new and old wine, Jesus told His critics that once old wine has been tasted, new wine is not appreciated (Luke 5:39). Old wine usually tastes better. The old religious ways may have seemed better, more comfortable; but in Jesus' parable, the old ways were not preferable. New thinking was needed for spiritual progress, but it was difficult for old thinkers to think in terms of new truths.

Pious Opposition

This kind of teaching only increased the hostility and criticism. The religious hierarchy must have seen Jesus as a revolutionary rabbi and a threat to their position in the status quo.

It comes as no surprise, then, that some of Jesus' most troublesome accusers were from the religious community. Ever eager to find a fresh accusation, they now focused their opposition on Jesus' views of their Sabbath-day practices. It all began with His next visit to Jerusalem for one of the annual festivals—probably the springtime Passover.

First, let's set the stage. Still visible today in Jerusalem are the remains of a famous structure from Jesus' time. In the Old City you can look down on several archways that are part of the five porches of what was called the Pool of Bethesda. It was a natural water supply and a place where people traditionally came for healing.

It was here on the Sabbath that Jesus restored a crippled man to health. Asking the man if he wanted to be made whole, Jesus told him to pick up the bedroll he was lying on and walk. Because he did just that, the religious leaders accused the man of working on the holy day by carrying his bed (John 5:6–10).

It was this kind of false piety—even blindness to human needs—that upset Jesus most. How could the hard-hearted Pharisees blithely ignore the fact that the man had been healed after 38 years of disability? They were obviously more concerned about their rules than about expressing joy at the man's recovery.

When they found out that it was Jesus who had helped the man, He became the target of their attack. As the Gospel writer John says, "because Jesus was doing these things on the Sabbath, the Jews persecuted him" (verse 16).

And when Jesus explained His thinking, things only got worse. He said, "My Father is always at his work to this very day, and I, too, am working." It was enough to choke them. In their opinion, Jesus had now made Himself equal with God. They felt they had no choice but to look for a way to kill Him and put an end to His outrageous remarks (verses 17–18).

The hostility to Jesus was now gaining such momentum that He would have to curtail His visits to Jerusalem for a time. But leaving Jerusalem didn't make questions about observance of the Sabbath day go away.

Lord of the Sabbath

As Jesus and His disciples made their way back to Galilee, they happened to stroll through a grain field on the seventh day. Some picked heads of grain to eat as they walked. According to three of the Gospel accounts, the watchful and fastidious Pharisees immediately accused them of breaking the Sabbath, this time by reaping crops (Matthew 12:1–2; Mark 2:23–24; Luke 6:1–2).

Jesus was quick to point out that the Sabbath was made for man, not man for the Sabbath. The Pharisees had made the day a burden instead of a delight. It was intended as a day of rest and worship, but they'd surrounded it with so many dos and don'ts that it was a hindrance to human life. Jesus cut through their ritualism; He was, He said, "Lord of the Sabbath" and therefore able to clarify its observance.

Later the same day Jesus visited a synagogue. There He found a man with a deformed hand. Again the Pharisees and the teachers of the law were watching. Again Jesus was prepared to challenge their rules and do a good work to heal the man.

The religious leaders were waiting to pounce, but Jesus confounded their arguments by asking whether it was lawful to do good on the Sabbath or to do harm. Didn't the law allow for an animal to be freed from a dangerous or difficult situation on the Sabbath? Then why not a human being (Matthew 12:9–13)?

This incident caused the Pharisees to find new allies in their opposition to Jesus. They joined ranks with another powerful political group—the active supporters of Herod known as the Herodians. Together the two groups now began to plot Jesus' death (Mark 3:6).

The situation was plainly getting much more dangerous. Jesus' popularity was increasing; His enemies knew it and feared it.

Not anxious to end His ministry yet, Jesus returned to the Sea of Galilee. But once He arrived back, people came to Him from all directions. He was now well known in Syria to the east, in Phoenicia to the west, to the southeast in Idumea—in fact, over an increasing span of the region.

It was time for Jesus to make an important decision for the future of His work. He prayerfully chose 12 from among His followers to become apostles. The care He took in the selection process is obvious from the account. We're told He went out and prayed all night about the choices He had to make (Luke 6:12–13).

"The Twelve" have been immortalized in Western culture. They were Simon Peter and his brother, Andrew; their partners in the fishing business, James and John, the sons of Zebedee; Philip; Bartholomew; Matthew the tax collector; Thomas; James, the son of Alphaeus; Simon the Zealot; Judas, also called Thaddaeus; and Judas Iscariot.

He chose these men to accompany Him in His work and also to go out themselves to preach and teach. In fact, the word *apostle* means "someone who is sent out." But before they could *be* sent out, Jesus had to train and teach them a great deal more.

Essential Teaching

In a place overlooking the Sea of Galilee, Jesus spent some time instructing His disciples about the fundamentals of the Way. What is popularly known as the Sermon on the Mount was the basis of that instruction.

There are two accounts in the New Testament of this core teaching. One is in chapters 5, 6 and 7 of Matthew's Gospel, the other in chapter 6 of Luke's. Although there are some differences between them, in the essentials they're the same. Some scholars feel they were two different, though parallel, sermons. Others believe it is one sermon recalled in slightly different ways.

The account begins with the familiar beatitudes, or blessings. These nine statements in Matthew 5:3–12 capture the essence of the godly frame of mind. They describe the kind of outlook and attitude followers of Jesus should have.

To say that these are godly values is to say that Jesus Christ Himself lived according to them. But they are, in fact, *universal spiritual truths*. And most of them echo earlier writings in the book of Psalms or the Prophets.

Jesus began: "Blessed are the poor in spirit, for theirs is the kingdom of heaven."

"The kingdom of heaven" is a phrase that's peculiar to Matthew's Gospel. Luke uses the similar "kingdom of God," and the meaning is equivalent. Whenever Jesus speaks about the totality of living under God's rule, Matthew uses "kingdom of heaven." It's code for the state of mind of a true disciple of Christ. It also anticipates the future kingdom of heaven to be set up on the earth. The disciples came to believe that Jesus would eventually return to the earth and set up that kingdom.

So in speaking the first beatitude, Jesus was demonstrating the benefit, or blessing, that a certain frame of mind produces in connection with the kingdom of God. In this case, the practice of *humility*—being small in our own eyes—results in entry into the kingdom of heaven.

As noted earlier, there are echoes of these thoughts elsewhere. In the prophet Isaiah's writings, we find a statement about God's appreciation of the humble spirit: "This is the one I esteem: he who is humble and contrite in spirit, and trembles at my word" (Isaiah 66:2b).

When humans come to themselves and gain perspective on the nature of their relationship with God, they cannot help but be humbled.

The lead-in to this passage in Isaiah helps the reader appreciate God's sovereignty: "This is what the LORD says: 'Heaven is my throne, and the earth is my footstool. Where is the house you will build for me? Where will my resting place be? Has not my hand made all these things, and so they came into being?' declares the LORD" (verses 1–2a).

When Jesus said, "Blessed are the poor in spirit"—the humble—He intended the kind of humility that is realistic, that appraises humanity's position in relation to His sovereignty. It's the beginning of a right relationship.

Blessed Are They

Another of the famous beatitudes or blessings pronounced by Christ is this one: "Blessed are those who mourn, for they will be comforted" (Matthew 5:4).

Spiritually speaking, here mourning is sorrow over the effects of sin. It leads to a repentant state of mind before God. It includes the recognition that ultimately sin is against God.

The Psalmist, David, said, "Against you [God], you only, have I sinned and done what is evil in your sight." He petitioned God, "Wash away all my iniquity and cleanse me from my sin" (Psalm 51:2–4). This signals a genuinely repentant attitude. In the Sermon on the Mount, we find that Jesus often drew the contrast between the genuine and the artificial, between true spirituality and human vanities, between the spirit of the law and the letter of the law, and between pleasing God and wanting to look good to our fellow human beings. A willingness to admit our sins and to turn from them is central to the meaning of repentance. It is a turning from wrong ways and returning to God's way as originally intended for humanity. How often have we done that?

Next in His discourse on the mountain, Jesus said, "Blessed are the meek, for they will inherit the earth" (Matthew 5:5). And here, perhaps, is the source of a common misconception. "Gentle Jesus, meek and mild," goes the children's Sunday school rhyme. The picture so often painted is of a soft, delicate Messiah—certainly not the former carpenter and stone mason who worked with His father around Nazareth. The concept of meekness, it seems, is much misunderstood.

Meekness is a quality denoting the quiet strength of teachability. A teachable spirit—one willing to learn—is a meek spirit. It is an extension of being poor in spirit, of humility. The result of such an attitude will be, according to Jesus, possession of the earth, or the land: "Blessed are the meek, for they will *inherit the earth*" (emphasis added).

In expressing this principle, Jesus was reiterating the same thought found in Psalm 37:11, which says "the meek will inherit the land and enjoy great peace." This is in contrast to "the wicked," who will "perish . . . vanish like smoke" (verse 20).

But *when* will that happen, you might ask. No doubt the listeners in Jesus' time asked the same. Clearly He was pointing to a future time—the time of the kingdom of heaven on earth; a time when Jesus Christ would be ruling in His kingdom on the earth; a time of future restoration.

Looking out on His disciples, Jesus continued: "Blessed are those who hunger and thirst for righteousness, for they will be filled" (Matthew 5:6). Jesus knew that only those who really search for the right ways to live with an unusual earnestness will gain such fulfillment. It requires a strong determination to seek out God's ways. The reward is great, because such people are going to have their desire for the right way to live before God fulfilled.

Next Jesus said: "Blessed are the merciful, for they will be shown mercy" (verse 7). We all want mercy when we are wrong or have done wrong. No one wants the penalty to be exacted; we all prefer to have another chance—but sometimes we are unwilling to extend that second chance to repentant others.

Jesus' words are very telling, cutting to the heart of our inadequacies, our meanness, our vindictive spirit: to obtain mercy, we must show mercy.

A category that Jesus emphasized next is those whose innermost being is honest and upright: "Blessed are the pure in heart." When we meet such people, we usually know it. The pure in heart have integrity. Their intentions are good, their faces are open, and such people, Jesus said, "will see God" (verse 8). Their reward will be closeness with God that is one of the richest of blessings.

Psalm 24:3–4 tells the story: "Who may ascend the hill of the LORD? Who may stand in his holy place? He who has clean hands and a pure heart. . . ."

A State of Mind

Next Jesus turned to the reconciliation of people: "Blessed are the peacemakers, for they will be called sons of God" (Matthew 5:9). God is a peacemaker. Strife, contention, disagreement—these are not the fruits of the mind of God at work. To be recognized as children of God, we have to practice the ways of God. One of them is peacemaking.

Of course, living in today's world, we're often challenged by the opposite spirit, the spirit of animosity and hostility. And that can lead to great pain. But Jesus taught, "Blessed are those who are persecuted because of righteousness" (verse 10). Inevitably in a society gone wrong—one that is running off the tracks—those who are trying to live by godly principles will experience opposition. But returning to the theme of the first blessing, Jesus said the persecuted will obtain "the kingdom of heaven."

In a postscript, He added that false accusation because of belief in Him shouldn't stop anyone. It is to be expected in a hostile world, but the result is God's blessing and a place in His kingdom.

The beatitudes—the blessings—summarize a state of mind that evidences humility, repentance, teachability, righteousness, mercy, pureness, peace, and patience in persecution. All of these characteristics are tied to a godly perspective and an assurance of a right and beneficial relationship with God.

This was just the beginning of Jesus' discourse. The entire message, though forgotten by most, is strikingly relevant today.

Chapter Three

First Things First

What Jesus was saying flew in the face of the false piety the Pharisees and religious leaders practiced. They claimed to observe the law of God and to be its teachers, but their interpretations and actions were in contradiction.

In Matthew's account of the Sermon on the Mount, Jesus moved from the beatitudes to a general description of the everyday, practical behavior of true followers. "You are the salt of the earth," He said to His disciples (Matthew 5:13).

This much-quoted verse points to the effect that the followers of Jesus are to have in their communities. They should be valuable participants, using their abilities and character traits to the full. They should be evident for their community involvement. Like salt's effect on food, Christ's followers are to enhance their social setting.

But then Jesus warned, "If the salt loses its saltiness, how can it be made salty again? It is no longer good for anything, except to be thrown out and trampled by men."

Salt was a valuable commodity in Jesus' time. But it could lose its value. And like salt that has lost its characteristic saltiness, Jesus said, disciples without visible good works are worthless. Tasteless salt is thrown away; that should not be the fate of Christ's followers.

Next, in three parallel statements to encourage action, Jesus said, "You are the light of the world." Then He added, "A city on a hill cannot be hidden," and finally, "Neither do people light a lamp and put it under a bowl" (verses 14–15).

These references to things that give out light and are seen tell us that the actions of Christ's followers should be the same; they should be visible. An oil lamp in the first century was, as Jesus said, put on a stand to give light to everyone in the house. The lesson became clear when Jesus added: "In the same way, let your light shine before men, that they may see your good deeds and praise your Father in heaven" (verse 16).

That is to say, in anything Christ-like people do, they should demonstrate the principles by which they live. It is not primarily by occasional acts of community service, but by living every day by Jesus' principles so that onlookers notice a difference. That means everyday followership, not a once-a-week show of allegiance. It is sincerity and truth in daily life.

What Jesus was saying flew in the face of the false piety the Pharisees and religious leaders practiced. They claimed to observe the law of God and to be its teachers, but their interpretations and actions were in contradiction.

A Law for Life

Jesus pointed out next that His purpose was to uphold and magnify the law of God, not make it of less effect. He said, "Do not think that I have come to abolish the Law or the Prophets; I have not come to abolish them but to fulfill them" (verse 17).

"The Law and the Prophets" comprise much of the Hebrew Scriptures—known by many as the Old Testament. *Old Testament* is an unfortunate phrase, because it privileges the New Testament in a way that can debase the value of the Scriptures that Jesus Christ Himself used to great effect in His teaching.

The *Old* part of the term *Old Testament* is simply a reference to the covenant relationship God established with ancient Israel at Mt. Sinai, when the Ten Commandments were given.

The *New* part of the phrase *New Testament* refers to the new relationship offered through Jesus Christ to all humanity. It includes access to the Father of humankind, through the gift of the Spirit of God. But it is a mistake to think of the Old Testament as redundant just because today we use the word *old* in describing it.

The Hebrew Scriptures were the basis of Jesus' teaching. He expanded on them, showing their deeper spiritual implications. He clearly valued them. And He said, "I tell you the truth, until heaven and earth disappear, not the smallest letter, not the least stroke of a pen, will by any means disappear from the Law until everything is accomplished" (verse 18).

There is authority in this statement—and it is unequivocal. Jesus could not have been plainer about the centrality of the law of God in human life.

Keeping the Law to the Letter

In Jesus' day, some of those who taught the law were Pharisees. If they were listening to the Sermon on the Mount, they heard a message that cut straight to the heart. On the other hand, if they would change their approach to God's commands, Jesus promised a significant future: "Whoever practices and teaches these commands will be called great in the kingdom of heaven," He said (verse 19).

Then, in a direct reference to the hypocrisy of some of the religious leadership, He added, "I tell you, that unless your righteousness surpasses that of the Pharisees and teachers of the law, you will certainly not enter the kingdom of heaven." These Pharisees and teachers were not living up to the deeper spiritual implications of the law; they were observing the letter but not the spirit of the law.

Next, Jesus showed His listeners the difference between observing the letter and living according to the spirit.

Speaking of commonly understood teachings about murder, adultery, swearing oaths, the treatment of enemies, divorce, and retaliation, He enlarged or magnified the implications of the law of God. For example, not only is the act of murder wrong, the attitude of anger and scorn behind it is also wrong. In such a frame of mind, a person cannot have a right relationship with God. First we must reconcile with our neighbor; only then will God hear us.

In the case of adultery, it is not just the sinful act that is wrong. Jesus specified the uncontrolled possessiveness prior to the act as equally wrong. He said, "Anyone who looks at a woman lustfully has already committed adultery with her in his heart" (verse 28).

In principle, of course, this is not a statement limited to men. A married person of either sex can have sexual desire for someone other than his or her partner. The point is that such temptations must be resisted if sin is to be avoided. Jesus was stressing that what goes on inside our heads is just as significant as the act of sin, because thought precedes action. Sin begins at the level of conscious thought. It ends in wrongful action.

The Divorce Debate

What about divorce? In the first-century Jewish world, it was a contentious issue from a religious perspective. The Jewish teachers were split over the grounds for divorce. There were conservative and liberal views. Some followed the teaching of the rabbi Shammai. He had said in an interpretation of the scriptural law that divorce was allowable only as a result of marital infidelity. He allowed no other reasons for such termination of marriage. His opponent in the debate over divorce was the rabbi Hillel. He had died seven or eight years before Jesus delivered the Sermon on the Mount. No doubt Hillel's teaching was popular, because he allowed divorce for just about any reason. Anything about the woman that displeased the man was ground for divorce in Hillel's opinion.

Jesus' purpose was to show the deeper spiritual implications of the law. He was going to uphold and fulfill the law—to show how it could and should be kept. He said, "Anyone who divorces his wife, except for marital unfaithfulness, causes her to become an adulteress, and anyone who marries the divorced woman commits adultery" (verse 32).

The undiluted strength of the young rabbi's teaching wasn't easy to take. His habit of getting to the heart of things was at once refreshing and challenging. He was obviously cut from different cloth than the traditional teachers.

Continuing, Jesus gave some teaching about the swearing of oaths. He said, "Let your 'Yes' be 'Yes,' and your 'No,' 'No'" (verse 37). He disagreed with the idea that swearing by heaven or earth or Jerusalem or anything else was necessary to ensure the fulfillment of a personal promise. What He stressed was the simple honesty of keeping one's word.

Going the Extra Mile

Has anything struck you about Jesus' teaching as we've looked at it? What is so impressive is His power to focus on the essential core of right human behavior.

The New Testament teaches that "the word of God is living and active. Sharper than any double-edged sword, it penetrates even to dividing soul and spirit, joints and marrow; it judges the thoughts and attitudes of the heart" (Hebrews 4:12)—a reason, perhaps, that many avoid it until there is nowhere else to go.

Jesus said that the principle of "eye for eye and tooth for tooth" was superseded by the principle of willing submission. It was an extremely hard saying. Some of Jesus' followers could not accept it. "But I tell you," He persisted, "Do not resist an evil person. If someone strikes you on the right cheek, turn to him the other also. And if someone wants to sue you and take your tunic, let him have your cloak as well. If someone forces you to go one mile, go with him two miles. Give to the one who asks you, and do not turn away from the one who wants to borrow from you" (Matthew 5:39–42).

Even enemies were included in this radical way of thinking. The hatred of enemies was gone, replaced by love and concern for them.

We are understandably impressed in the modern world by the extraordinary pacifist efforts of a Mahatma Gandhi or a Martin Luther King Jr. Their principles are found here in Jesus' own words; He said, "I tell you: Love your enemies and pray for those who persecute you, that you may be sons of your Father in heaven" (verses 44–45).

Like Father, Like Son

Jesus had a great purpose in all of this moral teaching: it was to enable human beings to take on godly characteristics. Summarizing, Jesus said, "You therefore must be [or become] perfect, as your heavenly Father is perfect" (verse 48, ESV).

It is important to remember in reading the Sermon on the Mount that Jesus was drawing a contrast between the practices of the religious authorities of His day and the reality of the true way of life He represented. What Jesus taught was daily practice anchored in sincerity, wholeheartedness and a complete devotion to God—nothing less. He knew, of course, that He was challenging teachers that had been compromised by politics and the corruptions of human nature.

When He spoke, His teaching was authoritative, penetrating and difficult to debate. At times He seemed radical; at others, reactionary. He reached forward with deeper insights, and backward in support of long-established truths. He expanded the old principles with fresh applications.

Face to Face

As He began the conclusion to His message, Jesus singled out the hypocrisy of those who professed religious belief and lived otherwise. In the Greek language of the New Testament, the word for "actor" has become our word *hypocrite*, meaning one who wears a mask, as the Greek actors did.

So when Jesus spoke of insincere acts of charity, prayer and fasting, He showed that it is possible to act out religious sentiments and be nothing more than a performer on a stage. Charitable acts, He said, should be done without show: "Be careful not to do your 'acts of righteousness' before men, to be seen by them. If you do, you will have no reward from your Father in heaven" (Matthew 6:1).

Apparently it was the practice of some, as they gave gifts at the temple in Jerusalem, to have a trumpet blown to attract attention to their charitable giving. That's why Jesus said: "When you give to the needy, do not announce it with trumpets, as the hypocrites do in the synagogues and on the streets, to be honored by men. I tell you the truth, they have received their reward in full" (verse 2)—that is, the acknowledgment of men but not of God. Jesus said such charitable works should be done in secret so that only God sees, and then He will reward accordingly.

Prayer, too, can be a vain show. "When you pray," He went on, "do not be like the hypocrites, for they love to pray standing in the synagogues and on the street corners to be seen by men. I tell you the truth, they have received their reward in full" (verse 5). Rather, Jesus taught that prayer should be a private communication with God. As recorded in the next verse, He said, "When you pray, go into your room, close the door and pray to your Father, who is unseen. Then your Father, who sees what is done in secret, will reward you."

He was clear, too, that hypocritical fasting should be avoided: "When you fast, do not look somber as the hypocrites do, for they disfigure their faces to show men they are fasting. I tell you the truth, they have received their reward in full. But when you fast, put oil on your head and wash your face, so that it will not be obvious to men that you are fasting, but only to your Father, who is unseen; and your Father, who sees what is done in secret, will reward you" (verses 16–18).

These were words that cut to the heart.

Right Priorities

In the next part of His discourse on primary values, Jesus turned to another subject that haunts our age: materialism. There are, He noted, more important riches than those found on earth.

The wealth He recommended was eternal and spiritual. He said, "Do not store up for yourselves treasures on earth, where moth and rust destroy, and where thieves break in and steal. But store up for yourselves treasures in heaven, where moth and rust do not destroy, and where thieves do not break in and steal" (verses 19–20).

When all is said and done, it is a matter of our primary focus of attention. If the heart is seduced by the appeal of materialism and riches now, then the important spiritual treasures will be ignored.

Jesus said it is impossible to be equally attached to God and to wealth. "No one can serve two masters," He said. "Either he will hate the one and love the other, or he will be devoted to the one and despise the other. You cannot serve both God and Money" (verse 24).

But if Jesus taught that material possessions are a diversion in life's spiritual quest, how are such everyday needs as food, clothing and shelter taken care of?

Jesus' answer was, as usual, straightforward. He said: "I tell you, do not worry about your life, what you will eat or drink; or about your body, what you will wear. Is not life more important than food, and the body more important than clothes? Look at the birds of the air; they do not sow or reap or store away in barns, and yet your heavenly Father feeds them. Are you not much more valuable than they?"

Worrying about the things that God knows we need is futile. "Why do you worry about clothes?" Jesus asked. "See how the lilies of the field grow. They do not labor or spin. Yet I tell you that not even Solomon in all his splendor was dressed like one of these. If that is how God clothes the grass of the field, which is here today and tomorrow is thrown into the fire, will he not much more clothe you, O you of little faith?" (verses 25–30).

The most important thing in life, He said, is to get our priorities right. Jesus put the capstone on this discussion of materialism with the words, "Seek first his kingdom and his righteousness, and all these [material] things will be given to you as well" (verse 33). That is a promise that requires faith on our part, and Jesus had much to say about faith.

Learn to Discern

In the final sections of the Sermon on the Mount, there is advice on godly and wise judgment, on how to find and retain truth, and on the need to heed Jesus' teaching.

The issue of making wise judgments includes not condemning others as long as we have our own problems to deal with. In other words, while we are all still human, Jesus said, we should not be so quick to condemn others for their failings. We all have our failings.

On the other hand, we must discern between right and wrong actions without condemning the individuals involved. So Jesus said: "Do not judge, or you too will be judged. For in the same way you judge others, you will be judged, and with the measure you use, it will be measured to you" (Matthew 7:1–2).

This kind of instruction is certainly serious; it carries an obvious gravity. But sometimes we have the impression that Jesus was only a "man of sorrows." Did He have a sense of humor? In this passage about judging others, He told us to take the plank out of our own eye before we try to rid our friend of the speck of dust in his or her eye. It is a humorous comment that demonstrates a vital principle.

But then Jesus immediately went on to say we should be sound in judgment. It's not that all judgment is to be avoided; for example, we should discern or judge to whom we should give spiritual truth. In the strongest terms, He said: "Do not give dogs what is sacred; do not throw your pearls to pigs. If you do, they may trample them under their feet, and then turn and tear you to pieces" (verse 6).

In the same way, He warned about false prophets or false teachers: "Watch out for false prophets. They come to you in sheep's clothing, but inwardly they are ferocious wolves" (verse 15).

It requires discernment, or judgment, to identify such impostors. So how can a person recognize false teachers?

Only by the effects of their words and actions: "By their fruit you will recognize them," Jesus explained. "Do people pick grapes from thornbushes, or figs from thistles? Likewise every good tree bears good fruit, but a bad tree bears bad fruit. A good tree cannot bear bad fruit, and a bad tree cannot bear good fruit. Every tree that does not bear good fruit is cut down and thrown into the fire. Thus, by their fruit you will recognize them" (verses 16–20). This is powerful encouragement to learn discernment.

To emphasize the deception that abounds when religious deceivers are active, Jesus continued: "Not everyone who says to me, 'Lord, Lord,' will enter the kingdom of heaven, but only he who does the will of my Father who is in heaven."

Even those who might claim allegiance to God's way could be left out in the final judgment. Jesus added, "Many will say to me on that day, 'Lord, Lord, did we not prophesy in your name, and in your name drive out demons and perform many miracles?' Then I will tell them plainly, 'I never knew you. Away from me, you evildoers!'" (verses 21–23).

When Jesus said these things, He was surrounded by spiritual charlatans, hypocrites, and selfish, politically motivated individuals. His message was a penetrating one: it is possible to *claim* to serve God, yet not be recognizable to Him.

Spiritual Truths

What was the antidote for such people? Stressing the need for earnestness and devotion of the wholehearted kind, Jesus said: "Ask and it will be given to you; seek and you will find; knock and the door will be opened to you. For everyone who asks receives; he who seeks finds; and to him who knocks, the door will be opened" (verses 7–8). God is a loving Father who will give His children everything they need.

In the same way that God shows outgoing concern for others, so should we. Jesus said, "So in everything, do to others what you would have them do to you, for this sums up the Law and the Prophets" (verse 12).

Jesus knew that living as His followers would be difficult in a secularized world and a world also fraught with religious antagonisms. That is the essence of His statement, recorded in verses 13 and 14: "Enter through the narrow gate. For wide is the gate and broad is the road that leads to destruction, and many enter through it. But small is the gate and narrow the road that leads to life, and only a few find it."

That clear image ties in with the final words of the sermon, which are an encouragement to heed Jesus' words: "Therefore everyone who hears these words of mine and puts them into practice is like a wise man who built his house on the rock" (verse 24). Then follows a parable about building on good foundations. Those who build on sand (the world's secular or pseudo-religious beliefs) will suffer great loss when the storms of life come. Those who build on the rock of Jesus' teaching, on the other hand, will cope best with the turbulence of life.

As Jesus completed His discourse, the people's reaction emphasized again the great difference between His instruction and that of their regular teachers. We read that "when Jesus had finished saying these things, the crowds were amazed at his teaching, because he taught as one who had authority, and not as their teachers of the law" (verses 28–29). Their teachers apparently quoted others to support their arguments. Jesus quoted nothing but the Scriptures themselves, reiterating their spiritual truths in His own words.

Here again, the importance of honesty and integrity in dealing with the Word of God and its principles is clear. Just as Jesus Himself was prepared to treat God's truth with complete sincerity, so must we. The value of the Word of God is for all to acknowledge: "For the word of God is living and active. Sharper than any double-edged sword, it penetrates even to dividing soul and spirit, joints and marrow; it judges the thoughts and attitudes of the heart" (Hebrews 4:12).

Universal Principles

What was it that made the Sermon on the Mount so memorable?

What Jesus gave were universal truths—principles that not only cut to the heart of human weakness but also showed the way ahead. Jesus spoke of those essential godly qualities that make our frail humanity surpassable: humility, for example—recognizing where we fit in the grand scheme of life—the relationship of human beings to God. He also explained how to gain forgiveness and to be forgiving, the importance of honest intentions, and the power of the peacemaker's frame of mind.

All of these aspects were reinforced with practical examples in Jesus' sermon. At times He was unrelenting in His description of how far we fall short of the spiritual standard God expects of us, of how easily we slip into playacting.

Chapter Four

Weighing the Evidence

"Go back and report to John what you have seen and heard: The blind receive sight, the lame walk, those who have leprosy are cured, the deaf hear, the dead are raised, and the good news is preached to the poor. Blessed is the man who does not fall away on account of me."

In a fascinating secular reference to Jesus, the pro-Roman Jewish historian Josephus, writing at the end of the first century, mentions Him as "a doer of wonders." It is the only early reference to His existence outside the New Testament.

To the 21st-century world, accounts of the wonders or miracles Jesus performed must surely be one of the more puzzling aspects of His ministry. The skeptical mind has to attempt explanations that cast a shadow over what is plainly and simply stated in the New Testament record. Of course, implied in the concept of *miracle* is that it is not open to rational explanation. What we do know is that after the end of Jesus' ministry, His followers were willing to die for what they believed about Him. Some of those same followers wrote of their own experiences as they witnessed His miraculous works.

At the conclusion of the Sermon on the Mount, as Jesus walked toward Capernaum, a small fishing village at the water's edge, a large crowd followed Him. Then, somewhere in the vicinity of the synagogue, the local Jewish leaders told Jesus about a very sick man who needed His help. The man happened to be the servant of a Roman centurion (Luke 7:1–3).

In an interesting aside about Roman-Jewish relations, we learn that the centurion had apparently built the Capernaum synagogue out of respect for the Jewish people. The black basalt foundations of that same synagogue may be what visitors see today when they tour the area.

On the way to visit the paralyzed man, messengers came to Jesus from the centurion. The centurion, they said, believed that he was unworthy of Jesus' visit and simply asked that Jesus say the word and his servant would be healed. Jesus now knew that it was not necessary to go any further. The centurion understood that Jesus had the authority to command sickness to depart, and that it would happen—rather like a Roman officer commanding his men to perform a task. His faith went beyond the need for Jesus to be physically present with his servant. It was a valuable lesson for all to understand.

The next day, at the small village of Nain on the plateau above Capernaum, another of Jesus' miracles caused the public to proclaim, "A great prophet has appeared among us," and "God has come to help his people." What Jesus saw as He approached the town was a funeral procession. A widow's only son had died. Jesus' compassion for the woman led Him to touch the coffin and raise the young man to life (verses 11–17).

This was the kind of miracle to bring a great deal of positive attention. Yet there was one man who was beginning to doubt Jesus.

The Baptist's Question

Surprisingly, we discover in Luke's narrative that John the Baptist, languishing in Herod's fortress prison, had begun to wonder about the legitimacy of Jesus' mission.

John's disciples had come to him with news of Jesus' growing work. John's response seems to show a troubled mind. Was he so despondent in prison that he had lost faith in Jesus, even though he had earlier announced Him as the Lamb of God, the One whose sandals he was not worthy to untie (John 1:26–31)?

John asked his disciples to go back and ask Jesus, "Are you the one who was to come, or should we expect someone else?" (Luke 7:18–19). Perhaps John was looking for a more immediate resolution of Roman oppression. Perhaps he thought Jesus should be a political messiah as well as a spiritual one.

When John's disciples asked his questions, Jesus' reply was straightforward. "Go back and report to John what you have seen and heard: The blind receive sight, the lame walk, those who have leprosy are cured, the deaf hear, the dead are raised, and the good news is preached to the poor. Blessed is the man who does not fall away on account of me." Jesus was saying that the miracles He performed by God's power provided some of the evidence of His Messiahship.

After John's disciples left, Jesus took the opportunity to explain to the crowds about the Baptist. He told them that John was a great prophet, one specified in the Scriptures as the messenger who would precede Jesus' own coming. He said John was a modern-day Elijah—one of ancient Israel's greatest prophets; but more than that, He said there had not been anyone greater than John the Baptist (verses 27–28; Matthew 11:11–14).

It was, of course, the ordinary people who had recognized the correctness of John's teaching. The Pharisees and experts in the law had not responded to his message of repentance and baptism. Jesus was displeased by this lack of right reaction to John.

Not to the Wise and Learned

John was not the only one whose message was going unheeded. Following in the footsteps of their forefathers, many who should have known better were rejecting the words and works of Jesus. In the Galilean towns of Bethsaida and Capernaum, for instance, Jesus had performed many of His miracles, and there had been little positive response from the wise and learned.

The village of Korazin in the hills above the Sea of Galilee was another place where the people knew Jesus. The remains of a synagogue, perhaps a successor to the one Jesus visited, are still there. Korazin was also one of the places that Jesus condemned for its lack of acceptance of His message. Today, black stone ruins are a stark reminder of its fate. As Jesus said, "If the miracles that were performed in you had been performed in Tyre and Sidon, they would have repented long ago in sackcloth and ashes. But I tell you, it will be more bearable for Tyre and Sidon on the day of judgment than for you" (Matthew 11:21–22).

Jesus' criticism of those considered wise and learned, and His recognition of the willing response of what He called "the little children," emphasized the uniqueness of His work. In the main, it was the ordinary folk who benefited from His teaching, not those filled with pride of position, power and intellect. Those burdened with life could find peace of mind. Those who saw their own need to learn were taught truth.

It wasn't long before another opportunity arose for Jesus to contrast the attitudes of the Pharisees and of the people. Jesus was eating dinner one evening in a Pharisee's home. A woman who had lived a sinful life came to the house to see Him (Luke 7:36–37). We're not told who she was or what her sins were. Speculation has it that she was a prostitute who had heard Jesus' message and now came to show her repentance.

She began to weep at Jesus' feet and poured perfume on them (verse 38). Attending to the feet was a servant's job; it was a mark of humility on the woman's part that she would do this, and symbolic of her deep remorse. Luke tells us that the woman wiped Jesus' feet with her hair, indicating that it was not tied up. This is somewhat unusual; a woman would normally have had her hair bound when in public. This may be a further indication of the woman's way of life.

The Pharisee, whose name was Simon, obviously did not approve of Jesus' tolerance of the woman. He thought to himself, Jesus cannot be a man of God or he would not let this kind of woman touch Him.

Jesus, perceiving Simon's attitude, said, "When I came to your house, you didn't offer water to wash My feet or greet Me with a kiss or anoint My head with oil. But this woman has wet My feet with her tears of repentance, kissed My feet and perfumed them. She has shown an attitude of great love and humility, and her many sins have been forgiven. In contrast, Simon, your lack of love and humility may mean you have been forgiven little, because you haven't sought God's forgiveness" (verses 44–47, paraphrased).

Rejected by His Own

Soon after this, Jesus began His second tour of the Galilean region, taking with Him His 12 disciples and certain women who supported them from their own means (Luke 8:1–3). Some of the women are mentioned by name.

One of them, Joanna, provides an interesting connection with the political culture of the time. She was the wife of a man named Cuza, who was manager of Herod

Antipas's household. It seems likely that such proximity to Herod would have allowed the king to know about Jesus' activities sooner or later. Herod's anxious involvement with the ministries of Jesus and John the Baptist is certainly a subtheme in the Gospel accounts.

But it was not only the political and religious leaders who worried about Jesus and His activities. Even His own family was concerned about Him, especially now that the crowds following Him were so great that at times He couldn't even eat (Mark 3:21).

As Jesus' miracles continued, however, the crowds began to speculate that He might be the Messiah, the son of David. The religious leadership, of course, rejected the thought and preferred instead the accusation that He was in league with the prince of demons, Beelzebub, or Satan. How often those who are doing right are vilified. Like the prophets of old, Jesus was suffering the rejection that is common to God's messengers.

Such contempt did not prevent Jesus from continuing to speak plainly. He pointed out to the legalists from Jerusalem that a house divided against itself cannot stand (verse 25). It made no sense to accuse Jesus of collusion with Satan when He was ridding the demon-possessed of their spirit tormentors. Rather, He warned the Pharisees to beware of accusing the Holy Spirit of evil; that, He said, is a sin that cannot be forgiven.

Drawing on the analogy of good fruit from good trees and bad fruit from bad ones, Jesus, like John the Baptist, characterized the hypocritical Pharisees as a brood of vipers unable to say anything good from the heart (Matthew 12:33–35).

Still, the scribes and Pharisees persisted in their ways, intent on trapping Jesus. They now asked for a miraculous sign (verse 38). Refusing their request, Jesus said that the only sign they would see would be the sign of the prophet Jonah, who spent three days and three nights in the belly of a huge fish. Referring to the Old Testament story of Jonah and his encounter with what has popularly become "the whale" (though the Bible does not specify a whale), Jesus spoke of His own death and His burial for three days and three nights in the tomb. The sign of His Messiahship was the fact that He would be in the heart of the earth for only three days and three nights.

The rejection of Jesus by the scribes and Pharisees only heightened His determination to make clear who was teaching truth and who was not.

At that moment, His mother and other family members arrived and asked for Him. His response was to make the point that the spiritual family (those who follow His way) is more important than the physical family (verses 46–50). So Jesus emphasized that in reality His mother and brothers are those who hear God's Word and put it into practice.

Obscuring Meaning

A little-known truth from the Gospel accounts is that in addressing the public, Jesus deliberately obscured His meaning on occasion. Contrary to popular opinion, telling a story in the form of a parable was one of Jesus' ways of hiding His point from the general public. It seems like a strange claim to make about the One who came as God's messenger to humanity. Why the apparent contradiction?

Here we will review a powerful series of eight parables that Jesus delivered regarding the kingdom of God. Four of the parables were given in public and four in private. The public parables were spoken from a boat anchored offshore in the Sea of Galilee so that the large crowds onshore could hear well. The private parables were given later in a house to the inner circle of disciples. The contrast between the two sets of messages provides the explanation as to why Jesus sometimes obscured the truth.

Take the first of the public parables, the famous story of a man sowing seed: "A farmer went out to sow his seed. As he was scattering the seed, some fell along the path, and the birds came and ate it up. Some fell on rocky places, where it did not have much soil. It sprang up quickly, because the soil was shallow. But when the sun came up, the plants were scorched, and they withered because they had no root. Other seed fell among thorns, which grew up and choked the plants. Still other seed fell on good soil, where it produced a crop—a hundred, sixty or thirty times what was sown. He who has ears, let him hear" (Matthew 13:3–9).

The audience listening on the seashore would have related easily to the everyday rural imagery. But did they grasp the spiritual implications of Jesus' words? Surprisingly, they were not intended to.

This is difficult to understand. Why speak in commonplace images if the audience was not meant to understand the spiritual significance? The answer becomes clear in a later conversation, when the disciples asked Jesus, "Why do you speak to the people in parables?" (verse 10).

Jesus' reply confirmed his intention, and it reveals a common misconception about the Bible. He said the reason He spoke to the public in parables was because "the knowledge of the secrets of the kingdom of heaven has been given to you, but not to them. . . . This is why I speak to them in parables: though seeing, they do not see; though hearing, they do not hear or understand" (verses 11 and 13).

Today we have access to Jesus' explanations because we can read them, but even now not all who read understand.

Seeds of Truth

When in subsequent private discussion with the disciples Jesus explained the spiritual message underlying the parable of the sower, He said that it was about hearing the truth. Some who hear truth don't value it; others hear it but get distracted along the way by the preoccupations of this life.

The parable of the sower also emphasized the importance of acting on the truth with enthusiasm and energy. "Listen then to what the parable of the sower means: When anyone hears the message about the kingdom and does not understand it, the evil one comes and snatches away what was sown in his heart. This is the seed sown along the path." Such a person hears but does not act on the truth he is hearing.

Next, "the one who received the seed that fell on rocky places is the man who hears the word and at once receives it with joy. But since he has no root, he lasts only a short time." Such a person permits personal difficulties to overcome early understanding of truth. "When trouble or persecution comes because of the word, he quickly falls away."

Then there's the person who lets the preoccupations of life get in the way of truth: "The one who received the seed that fell among the thorns is the man who hears the word, but the worries of this life and the deceitfulness of wealth choke it, making it unfruitful."

Finally, the person "who received the seed that fell on good soil is the man who hears the word and understands it. He produces a crop, yielding a hundred, sixty or thirty times what was sown" (verses 18–23). From this we can see that the future kingdom of heaven will begin with those who pursue and practice spiritual truth in this life.

The Gospel author Mark has recorded an additional part of this parable about seed as it grows. Quoting Jesus, he writes, "This is what the kingdom of God is like. A man scatters seed on the ground. Night and day, whether he sleeps or gets up, the seed sprouts and grows, though he does not know how. All by itself the soil produces grain—first the stalk, then the head, then the full kernel in the head. As soon as the grain is ripe, he puts the sickle to it, because the harvest has come" (Mark 4:26–29).

This tells us that the follower of Jesus Christ is committed to the development of spiritual character now for the coming kingdom of God—a lifelong, continually developing spiritual growth to be harvested for good use by God.

Planted by the Enemy

In the second parable of the first set of four related by Matthew, Jesus explained that "the kingdom of heaven is like a man who sowed good seed in his field. But while everyone was sleeping, his enemy came and sowed weeds among the wheat, and went away. When the wheat sprouted and formed heads, then the weeds also appeared.

The owner's servants came to him and said, 'Sir, didn't you sow good seed in your field? Where then did the weeds come from?' 'An enemy did this,' he replied. The servants asked him, 'Do you want us to go and pull them up?' 'No,' he answered, 'because while you are pulling the weeds, you may root up the wheat with them. Let both grow together until the harvest. At that time I will tell the harvesters: First collect the weeds and tie them in bundles to be burned; then gather the wheat and bring it into my barn'" (Matthew 13:24–30).

Once again the people on the seashore heard an interesting agrarian analogy. But again the deeper significance was not evident to them. This is obvious from the account, when later in the house even the disciples asked for clarification.

Explaining, Jesus said: "The one who sowed the good seed is the Son of Man. The field is the world, and the good seed stands for the sons of the kingdom. The weeds are the sons of the evil one, and the enemy who sows them is the devil. The harvest is the end of the age, and the harvesters are angels. As the weeds are pulled up and burned in the fire, so it will be at the end of the age. The Son of Man will send out his angels, and they will weed out of his kingdom everything that causes sin and all who do evil. They will throw them into the fiery furnace, where there will be weeping and gnashing of teeth. Then the righteous will shine like the sun in the kingdom of their Father. He who has ears, let him hear" (verses 37–43).

This is a very clear overview of Jesus' teaching about eternal life. But, He warned, there is an enemy, Satan the devil, who tries to disrupt the development of the true followers of Christ. He does this by surrounding them with lawless behavior in an effort to choke them off from right action. At the end, in the judgment, the righteous who have not been deterred will gain eternal life in the kingdom of God to be established on the earth.

Jesus' third public parable was about a very small seed: "The kingdom of heaven is like a mustard seed, which a man took and planted in his field. Though it is the smallest of all your seeds, yet when it grows, it is the largest of garden plants and becomes a tree, so that the birds of the air come and perch in its branches" (verses 31–32).

The hidden message here is that the kingdom of heaven starts out very small in this age and grows to encompass the whole earth in God's future society on earth.

A similar principle is covered in the fourth and final parable to the public, the parable of the leaven, or yeast: "The kingdom of heaven is like yeast that a woman took and mixed into a large amount of flour until it worked all through the dough" (verse 33).

This is a picture of the transformation of human beings and the continual spread of the kingdom of God, like yeast permeates dough to make bread rise. It is a kingdom that begins in this life with the believer and finds its next great fulfillment in the coming of Jesus Christ to reign on the earth.

Buried Treasure

After these four parables, Jesus left the crowds and went back to His house in Capernaum. It was there, alone with His disciples, that He gave the final set of four parables: the parable of the hidden treasure, the parable of the pearl of great price, the parable of the net, and the parable of the householder's treasure.

The first one says: "The kingdom of heaven is like treasure hidden in a field. When a man found it, he hid it again, and then in his joy went and sold all he had and bought that field" (verse 44). It is an analogy to teach that the kingdom of God is something of unsurpassed value for which no sacrifice is too great.

The next parable makes a similar point: "Again, the kingdom of heaven is like a merchant looking for fine pearls. When he found one of great value, he went away and sold everything he had and bought it" (verses 45–46). Just as a merchant trading in fine jewelry looks for the very best, nothing should prevent the believer in his quest for the priceless truth, and having found it, he should treasure it above all else.

The third parable given inside the house was about the good and the bad existing side by side in the world until the judgment: "Once again, the kingdom of heaven is like a net that was let down into the lake and caught all kinds of fish. When it was full, the fishermen pulled it up on the shore. Then they sat down and collected the good fish in baskets, but threw the bad away. This is how it will be at the end of the age. The angels will come and separate the wicked from the righteous and throw them into the fiery furnace, where there will be weeping and gnashing of teeth" (verses 47–50).

The final parable pictured the knowledge of the kingdom of God as the private treasure of those faithful in this life: "He said to them, 'Therefore every teacher of the law who has been instructed about the kingdom of heaven is like the owner of a house who brings out of his storeroom new treasures as well as old'" (verse 52). This is a description of the person who has recognized the truths that lead to a life that is pleasing to God, the person who presses on toward the kingdom of God, delighting in the priceless, newly discovered treasure.

Matthew's account of this concise set of parables shows Jesus teaching His disciples truths that the majority of the public could not appreciate—spiritual gems. But He also taught that it was the duty of those who could understand to hold on to such truths with all of their being. They would experience the values and promises of God and live a successful, godly life. They would also have an expectation of the kingdom of God ruling over the whole earth.

Parables and Parallels

Now let's pause a moment and recap, because there is an impressive pattern in the parables of Matthew 13.

Take the first and last parables together: the first, outside by the sea, was the parable of the sower—a public message about receiving the truth. The last, inside the house, was the parable of the householder's treasure—a private message about receiving the truth.

Then, again outside by the sea, was the parable of the tares, or weeds, picturing the good and the bad developing together, to be separated at the judgment. Inside the house, Jesus gave the parable of the net—the good and the bad caught together, again to be separated at the judgment.

Next to last outside by the sea was the parable of the mustard seed, a single object representing the kingdom. Inside the house again, the parable of the pearl; once more, a single object representing the kingdom.

And the final parallel: outside by the sea, the parable of the yeast, which is hidden material. And inside, the parable of the treasure in the field; again, hidden material.

There is a remarkable symmetry to this pattern of the parables, found mostly in Matthew's Gospel but certainly echoed in the other Gospel accounts. These eight parables reveal a great deal about the coming kingdom of God on earth. That kingdom was the heart and core of Jesus' message, yet so few today understand it or anticipate it.

Chapter Five

The Way of Transformation

Our ultimate destiny as human beings is to become the resurrected children of God living life eternally in a renewed world. That means we must take on the nature and moral character of the family of God.

Jesus had spent the day, as He often did, before a crowd of people who had gathered to hear His unusually authoritative words.

At evening time, He and His disciples set out to cross over the Sea of Galilee to escape the crowds, and Jesus quickly fell asleep in the small boat. When a sudden storm came on them, the disciples began to panic, fearful of drowning. They awakened Jesus, who, surprised by their lack of faith, calmed the winds and the waves.

It was an impressive miracle to convince the disciples of His power over the elements. Despite a long day of learning about the kingdom of God, they still were not sure enough of their leader to trust Him in a storm at sea. The miraculous calming of the storm perhaps helped them confirm their belief.

Once across the turbulent sea, they arrived at Gerasa on the eastern shore, nine miles south of Capernaum. Gerasa was home to two men who were possessed by a multitude of demons. The men came out of the tombs where they apparently lived. Like many under the influence of evil spirits, one of them was strong enough to tear off his restraining chains. Jesus' arrival obviously upset the two men. But He simply commanded the evil spirits to leave them. The spirits asked to enter a herd of 2,000 pigs feeding on the nearby hillside. When the demons came into contact with the herd, the pigs ran over the cliff into the sea and drowned.

Understandably, their herdsmen were angry and went into town to report what had happened. The townspeople came to see for themselves and found Jesus with one of the formerly demon-possessed men, now in his right mind (Matthew 8:28–34; Mark 5:1–17; Luke 8:26–37).

Because of the loss of the pigs, the local people asked Jesus to leave. Getting into a boat, Jesus refused passage to the now sane man. Rather, He said, go and tell your family what has happened (Mark 5:18–20; Luke 8:38–39).

The men from whom the bad spirits had disappeared went home and explained what had happened to them. As a result, Jesus' fame spread throughout the 10-city region of Decapolis, east of the Jordan River.

Faith Found and Faith Failed

When Jesus arrived back at the western side of the Sea of Galilee, a large crowd met Him. Among them was a synagogue ruler named Jairus, probably a leader of the Capernaum congregation. His daughter was very ill, and he asked Jesus for help.

On His way to visit the young girl, a dense crowd surrounded Jesus so that it was impossible for Him to move without brushing up against others. When Jesus suddenly asked who had touched Him, it seemed a strange question to His disciples, and an impossible one to answer. But Jesus' reason for asking was that He had felt power leave Him, as He said.

At that moment, a woman came forward to admit she had touched Him trusting that she would be healed of a 12-year illness. The remarkable part of her admission was that she had indeed been healed instantly. Jesus said that her faith had saved her (Mark 5:21–34).

This incident on the way to help Jairus's daughter was strong evidence to the synagogue ruler. But the noisy crowd at Jairus's house was in a different mood. They laughed out loud when Jesus said the now dead girl was only sleeping.

Their scornful laughter turned to amazement when Jesus addressed the little girl and simply said, "Get up," and she did. Unlike His earlier instruction to the men who had been demon possessed, Jesus charged the girl and her parents to say nothing about the miracle—now that He was back in Galilee (verses 35–43).

After helping Jairus and his daughter, Jesus next healed two blind men who came to Him. He warned them, too, against publicizing the miracle of their newly restored sight. But their exuberance overcame them, and they told everyone in the region.

At the same time, Jesus also healed a demon-possessed man who was unable to speak. The crowds were astonished. "Nothing like this has ever been seen in Israel," they said (Matthew 9:27–33). But the Pharisees said it was sorcery.

Shortly after this incident, Jesus returned to His hometown of Nazareth for one final visit. He had already been rejected by His fellow townspeople as He began His work. Now He taught once again in the same synagogue. But in contrast to recent events, He could perform no miracles there, because His former neighbors and acquaintances lacked faith in the familiar son of Joseph. "'Isn't this the carpenter's son? Isn't his mother's name Mary, and aren't his brothers James, Joseph, Simon and Judas? . . . Where then did this man get all these things?' And they took offense at him" (Matthew 13:55–57).

Special Calling

As we are seeing, Jesus' work brought one of two responses: either outright rejection or amazement. Did miracles convince anyone to adopt Jesus' teachings? The Gospel accounts do not tell us directly. But it is apparent that discipleship was a calling, not a decision based on witnessing miracles. Miracles may have been an adjunct to belief, but they were not the cause of discipleship. Even Jesus' own family had difficulty accepting His unique powers and authority. But His 12 disciples demonstrated an unusual willingness to give up all and follow their leader. They would come to understand later that this was a special calling that came only through the intervention of the Holy Spirit—a gift that God ultimately gives to those who change their mindset and follow His way. The disciples' conviction was something that allowed them to serve Jesus effectively.

Sensing that His mission could now be expanded, Jesus called the twelve together and commissioned them to go out in parties of two to preach and heal as He had been doing. But He warned them of the opposition they would face immediately and in the long term: "I am sending you out like sheep among wolves. Therefore be as shrewd as snakes and as innocent as doves" (Matthew 10:16).

The price of discipleship was high. The twelve would teach as Jesus had done and receive both enthusiastic support and bitter opposition. Jesus, quoting the prophet Micah, said of His own mission, "Do not suppose that I have come to bring peace to the earth. I did not come to bring peace, but a sword. For I have come to turn 'a man against his father, a daughter against her mother, a daughter-in-law against her mother-in-law—a man's enemies will be the members of his own household'" (verses 34–36).

These were strong words indeed, and not what we normally associate with the Teacher from Nazareth. What exactly did He mean?

As Jesus explained in detail, it is a matter of profound commitment. He said: "Anyone who loves his father or mother more than me is not worthy of me; anyone who loves his son or daughter more than me is not worthy of me; and anyone who does not take his cross and follow me is not worthy of me. Whoever finds his life will lose it, and whoever loses his life for my sake will find it" (verses 37–39). It was a difficult but fair exchange.

A Queen Gets Revenge

While the 12 disciples went on their Galilean journey, Jesus, too, continued to teach and travel. Needless to say, such widespread public activities brought the attention of King Herod Antipas himself.

It's at this point that the Gospel narrative relates how Herod was forced to resolve his impasse with John the Baptist. The story is perhaps familiar, but the details provide a fascinating look at the corrupt king's lifestyle and the reality of conducting any publicly acclaimed work in his territory.

As we noted earlier, according to the first-century Jewish historian Josephus, it was at Machaerus, Herod's hilltop fortress in present-day Jordan, that the king imprisoned John the Baptist. But the scene we are about to recount probably occurred in Tiberias, by the Sea of Galilee. It was there that Herod Antipas had built his new palace.

To recap the story a little, Herod had taken his brother's wife in an adulterous and incestuous relationship. John had criticized him publicly for this as well as for various other corrupt activities. But Herod was unwilling to kill John because he was fascinated with the man's message. He simply liked to listen to him.

Herod's wife, Herodias, had a daughter who danced for the king. Josephus tells us that her name was Salome, though the Bible is silent on this. Her dancing was apparently sexually pleasing to Herod. At his birthday celebration with various officials, military commanders and Galilean leaders, he promised up to half his kingdom to the girl if she would dance for them. In fact, she could ask for anything she wanted up to that value. The girl danced, and Herod asked what she wanted in return. She consulted her mother for advice. Her mother's anger at John the Baptist's moral condemnation of her marriage led her to request John's head on a platter.

The girl told Herod and, unwilling to face humiliation before his guests, he agreed. So it was that John was beheaded at the whim of a vicious queen and through the weakness of a compromised king. John's head was delivered on a plate as requested (Mark 6:17–28).

His disciples soon came to remove his body for burial—an indication that the murder probably took place in Tiberias.

No sooner had Herod killed John than he began to hear of Jesus' growing work and popularity. The Gospel writers record Herod's reaction as thinking John the Baptist had returned from the dead in the form of Jesus. Herod was also hearing reports that John was Elijah or one of the ancient prophets come back to life (verses 14–16). Herod's perplexity caused him to try to see Jesus. From this point Jesus' contact with the public would become less frequent.

Less Is More

Careful to preserve His freedom for a while longer, Jesus and His disciples went by boat to Bethsaida-Julias, a small town at the northern end of the lake. Today it is the site of a beautiful nature reserve shaded by eucalyptus trees and intersected by several streams, all part of the Jordan as it flows into the Sea of Galilee.

In this area the twelve and their Master sought some rest. But it was not to be. As they got out of the boat, a crowd that had gone ahead met them. Jesus, feeling great compassion for these sheep without a shepherd, taught them about the kingdom of God and healed those who needed help. It was typical of Jesus that He would often set aside His own needs and serve others freely.

The day wore on, and by evening the crowds, now numbering about 5,000 men *plus* women and children, were hungry. The disciples asked Jesus to send the people away so that they could buy something to eat in the surrounding villages. Jesus' reply was a test of a kind. He said to Philip, "Where shall we buy bread for these people to eat?" As the Gospel of John says, "He asked this only to test him, for he already had in mind what he was going to do" (John 6:5–6). Philip's response was that it would take more than eight months' wages to buy enough bread for each one to have a bite.

What Jesus had in mind, of course, was one of the most well-known miracles—the feeding of up to 15,000 people with only five small barley loaves and two small fish provided by a boy in the crowd. Looking up, Jesus gave thanks over the small amount of food. He then simply distributed as much as anyone wanted. At the end of the meal the disciples collected 12 baskets of leftover food (Mark 6:35–44).

Perhaps this miracle was as much for the disciples as for the hungry crowds. They really needed to develop unshakable confidence in their Master. Though they would go through a crisis of faith in the near future, these experiences would form the basis of their later work as apostles.

Another Lesson in Faith

Once the people were fed, Jesus sent the disciples back by boat to another village named Bethsaida, on the western shore near Capernaum. He then dismissed the crowd, which was ready to make Him a king or political messiah by force, and went to the mountain alone to pray.

Several hours later, in the midst of a windstorm on the lake, Jesus came to His disciples' boat in a miraculous way. They had been fighting the storm for some hours. Remember that several of them were fishermen who knew the Sea of Galilee well. They had been rowing, straining at the oars. In the middle of the night they saw a figure coming toward them across the water. Terrified, they shouted out, "It's a ghost!" (verses 47–50).

Jesus, walking on the water, said, "Take courage! It is I. Don't be afraid."

The impetuous Peter wanted to get out of the boat and walk to Jesus. When Jesus told him, "Come," he did. But after a few brave steps Peter began to sink, afraid of the storm. Jesus grasped his hand and saved him, taking him safely back to the boat (Matthew 14:22–31).

Once again the wind died down, as it had in a previous storm on the lake when the disciples were afraid. All of this was more stunning evidence of why the disciples should have faith in their Master. Mark's Gospel points out that the disciples were amazed, because they had failed to grasp the significance of the feeding of the great crowd (Mark 6:51).

Soon they were back on shore near Capernaum. As they landed, the people recognized Jesus and spread the word that the man who could heal was back. They hoped to just touch the edge of His garment and so to be made well.

The Bread of Life

The next day, while the feeding of the thousands was still fresh in people's minds, Jesus took the opportunity to explain the importance of finding bread that truly satisfies.

He said to the crowd, "I tell you the truth, you are looking for me, not because you saw miraculous signs but because you ate the loaves and had your fill" (John 6:26). It was, in fact, not because of the spiritual aspects of Jesus' work that they were seeking Him, but because of something as physical as food in the stomach. He said they should be searching for food that would feed them spiritually and bring them closer to eternal life. The crowds immediately wanted to know what it was that would bring God's favor. Jesus told them they should believe the One whom God had sent.

Part of the problem is that we humans so often do not believe what God says and does. We would rather express confidence in man than in what God does. Yet God says, "Cursed is the one who trusts in man, who depends on flesh for his strength and whose heart turns away from the LORD" (Jeremiah 17:5).

Jesus' listeners asked next for a miraculous sign so that they could believe in Him—an amazing request, because evidently some of them had been present the day before when He had fed the huge crowd. They said that Moses had given their forefathers bread, or manna, from heaven—the implication being that He should now do the same.

Jesus told them that it was not Moses but God Himself who had given the true bread from heaven. That bread He was about to reveal (John 6:30–33).

Like the Samaritan woman at the well who wanted the water of life (John 4:15), these people now wanted the bread of life. They said in response, "From now on give us this bread."

It was then that Jesus announced to them that He was "the bread of life" (John 6:35, 48). The implications of the statement are profound. Perhaps that is why at the end of the discussion many of His own followers said, "This is a hard teaching. Who can accept it?"

Joseph's Son or Son of God?

What was Jesus' point? Simply this: Without making His way an integral part of our lives, we will never be like the Father or the Son. Our ultimate destiny as human beings is to become the resurrected children of God living life eternally in a renewed world. That means we must take on the nature and moral character of the family of God. The only way that can be done is as Jesus said in His analogy: we must partake of the nature of God.

Jesus made it clear that only some are called now. He said plainly that no one can come to Him—to accept Him as the Son of God—unless the Father actually draws that person (verse 44). It is an act on the part of the Father that brings a person to a willingness to follow Jesus Christ. This action by the Father is not something that is generally understood.

Some of Jesus' listeners began to grumble because He said that He had come down from heaven as the bread of heaven. They could see Him only as Joseph's son. He was the young man whose parents they knew. In this case their familiarity with Him led to disbelief.

Jesus simply repeated the same idea that those whom God is calling will understand; others will not. He said that He was the bread of life. Connecting this with His coming sacrificial death, He said, "This bread is my flesh, which I will give for the life of the world" (verse 51). He explained that we must partake of Him. Christ has to become a part of every true follower, and the resulting transformation of human nature will lead to eternal life.

It was a difficult and profound teaching, and many disciples left Jesus that day. The twelve did not (verses 66–69). They had come to believe that, as Peter said, "you are the Holy One of God."

Clean Hands, Clean Heart

Next, the scribes and the Pharisees were about to have a lesson about playacting spirituality.

They had tried to entrap Jesus over Sabbath observance, saying that He was breaking the rules. He had shown them that it is the law of God about the Sabbath that must be kept, not the laws invented by man to surround it.

Now the scribes and Pharisees were in Galilee trying once more to catch the Teacher off guard. This time their questions dealt with the Jewish practice of ritual hand washing before eating. It was the custom of the strict religious parties to wash up to the elbows before eating. Only then were they ritually clean.

When they asked why Jesus' disciples did not follow this tradition of the elders, He told them that they were fulfilling a prophecy of Isaiah, which said, "These people draw near with their mouths and honor Me with their lips, but have removed their hearts far from Me, and their fear toward Me is taught by the commandment of men" (Isaiah 29:13, NKJV). In other words, the law of God was being obscured by the tradition of men.

To demonstrate the point, Jesus said: "You have a fine way of setting aside the commands of God in order to observe your own traditions! For Moses said, 'Honor your father and your mother'. . . . But you say that if a man says to his father or mother, 'Whatever help you might otherwise have received from me is Corban' (that is, a gift devoted to God), then you no longer let him do anything for his father or mother. Thus you nullify the word of God by your tradition that you have handed down" (Mark 7:9–13; Matthew 15:3–6).

What Jesus was objecting to was their means of circumventing the clear responsibility of children toward their parents as prescribed in the law. So once again we see that it is so easy for human beings to think they are being religious, even pleasing God, when they are doing the exact opposite of what His law requires. The heart is where God's interest lies, as Jesus went on to show.

He said that it is not what goes into a person that makes him unclean, but rather what comes from the innermost being. This passage is often mistakenly thought to mean that we can eat anything, including what the Bible says is unclean. But it's clear from the context that Jesus' point related to human motivation, not food. The subject under discussion was not whether a person should eat pork or shellfish, but what comes from the human heart.

He concluded His remarks this way: "What comes out of a man, that defiles a man. For from within, out of the heart of men, proceed evil thoughts, adulteries, fornications, murders, thefts, covetousness, wickedness, deceit, lewdness, an evil eye, blasphemy, pride, foolishness. All these evil things come from within and defile a man" (Mark 7:20–23, NKJV).

The subject of clean and unclean food is an interesting one, of course. It is often thought that Jesus did not believe in keeping the Bible's food laws. This is an illogical conclusion. He was, after all, born into an observant Jewish family. We read that His parents raised Him according to the ways of God, that He was obedient to them, and that He grew in favor with God and man. There is no evidence that He was disobedient to the laws of God. He said, "Do not think that I have come to abolish the Law or the Prophets" (Matthew 5:17).

The scribes and the Pharisees would have had a case to make if Jesus and the disciples were eating unclean foods, but the issue they raised was about ritual washing according to their human traditions. They never raised a question about what the disciples ate.

The Miracle Worker

Sometimes Jesus traveled outside the territory of Judea and Galilee—for example, to the Mediterranean seacoast cities of Tyre and Sidon in what is Lebanon today. Jesus went there with His disciples and tried to keep His presence secret, but it was impossible. Soon a Greek woman from Syrian Phoenicia approached Him. She begged that her daughter be healed of demon possession (Mark 7:24–26).

Jesus knew that His immediate mission was to the children of Israel. He did not respond to the woman until she demonstrated her understanding of God's relationship to Israel. Her humble admission that it was only indirectly at that time, by contact with Israel, that the gentile peoples were to be blessed, convinced Christ that she did understand. He healed her daughter at a distance. When the woman returned home, she found her daughter in a normal frame of mind (Matthew 15:21–28).

Next, Jesus and His disciples went to the eastern side of the Sea of Galilee and the 10 Greek cities of the Decapolis, where He healed a man who could not hear and who could barely speak. He told the crowd who witnessed this not to tell anyone. That proved difficult, and the more He asked them not to, the more they spread the word. In the end, great crowds came to see Him in the area southeast of the Sea of Galilee (verses 29–31; Mark 7:31–37).

At this point in the Gospel account we find Jesus repeating a miraculous event that had occurred only recently with another large crowd. Jesus said to His disciples: "I have compassion for these people; they have already been with me three days and have nothing to eat. If I send them home hungry, they will collapse on the way, because some of them have come a long distance" (Mark 8:2–3).

Finding that the disciples had seven loaves and a few small fish, He asked God's blessing on the food and fed 4,000 men, plus women and children. This was the second time that He had fed multiple thousands miraculously (verses 18–20). As before, the disciples picked up several baskets of scraps at the end of the meal.

After this Jesus went back to Galilee, only to be met by hostile questioning. Now the Sadducees, another religious party, joined the Pharisees in their criticism of Jesus.

This time the critics were asking Him for a sign from heaven. He told them that the signs they did see from heaven on a regular basis, like a red sky at night or in the morning, seemed to present them with no difficulty. They could understand that certain weather was on the way when they saw such signs. Yet when they saw the works of Christ, they couldn't recognize them but wanted some other miraculous display.

Jesus said they would see no other sign than the sign of the prophet Jonah (Matthew 16:1–4). He had told them this very same thing earlier in His travels. Jonah was three days and three nights in the belly of a great fish, symbolic of Christ's three days and three nights in the tomb after His crucifixion.

Going back across the lake, Jesus took the opportunity to instruct His disciples about the teaching of the Pharisees, the Sadducees and the Herodians. He compared all three parties to leaven, or yeast, the effect of which spreads quickly in dough. He warned His disciples that wrong teaching spreads quickly too.

The disciples at first didn't grasp Jesus' meaning when He said, "Watch out for the yeast of the Pharisees" (Mark 8:15). They thought He was speaking about the fact that they had brought no bread with them. When He reminded them that He had been able to provide enough food for thousands of people on two recent occasions, they realized that He was speaking of something quite different.

Landing at the northern shore near Bethsaida-Julias, Jesus healed a blind man, telling him to say nothing in his village but to simply go home. Once again Jesus sought to avoid public attention (verses 22–26).

A New Phase Begins

Next we follow Jesus' footsteps to Caesarea Philippi in the northern part of the territory of Israel, beyond the jurisdiction of Herod Antipas. This was the territory of his half brother Philip, who didn't have the same suspicions about Jesus. His territory was populated by gentile peoples who would not have had such antagonism to Jesus as the Jewish religious parties did.

Surrounded by His disciples, Jesus now began to probe their understanding about His own role and responsibility. He asked, "Who do people say the Son of Man is?" They replied, "Some say John the Baptist; others say Elijah; and still others, Jeremiah or one of the prophets." He pressed them: "But what about you? Who do you say I am?" Peter replied, "You are the Christ, the Son of the living God" (Matthew 16:13–16).

This was the beginning of a real recognition of Jesus' unique identity by the disciples. They had been in Jesus' company for some time. They had witnessed many miraculous events that strained their normal capacity for disbelief. The evidence that this was no ordinary man had become overwhelming; not even charisma could account for the extraordinary things He said and did.

It was not by human reasoning that they came to accept Jesus as the Son of God. Jesus made that clear when He said, "Blessed are you, Simon son of Jonah, for this was not revealed to you by man, but by my Father in heaven" (verse 17).

It was a significant part of Jesus' teaching that no one can accept Him unless the Father causes a change in the normal human perspective. Jesus had made that plain to

His Jewish audiences more than once before. Here again He stressed that a revelation from the Father was necessary to understand that He was the Christ to come.

Jesus went on to make a prophetic statement about the founding of the New Testament Church. He said to Peter, "I tell you that you are Peter, and on this rock I will build my church, and the gates of Hades will not overcome it. I will give you the keys of the kingdom of heaven; whatever you bind on earth will be bound in heaven, and whatever you loose on earth will be loosed in heaven" (verses 18–19).

This has been commonly understood to indicate Peter's leadership over the Church as it developed after Christ's death. Certainly Peter would have an important role to play. There is something to be learned, however, from the different Greek words used here. When Jesus said, "You are Peter," He used the masculine form, *petros*, which means a rock or a stone. When He said, ". . . and on this rock I will build my church," He used the feminine form, *petra*, which means a large stone, a rock, a cliff, a ledge, a crag. It is understood that by the second rock Christ was referring to Himself. He was the rock on which the Church would be built.

Peter was to be given the keys to the kingdom; that is, certain authority symbolized by keys. The apostles would ultimately have authority in the Church to guide it under Christ toward the kingdom of God.

Having introduced these new concepts, including the fact that there would be a church, Jesus strictly warned His disciples not to tell anyone else what they had recognized about Him. This episode marks the beginning of a new phase in Jesus' disclosure of His purpose.

"The Things of God"

Next, Jesus had to prepare His disciples for His certain death at Jerusalem and His resurrection on the third day. This was difficult to understand, let alone accept. Peter's response was to rebuke Jesus for saying that He would be killed. He said, "Never, Lord! This shall never happen to you!"

Jesus had to rebuke Peter in return, reminding him that he was acting under the sway of the evil one to say such things. Jesus used the same language in addressing Peter that He had used in the temptation battle between Himself and Satan. He said to Peter, "Get behind me, Satan! You are a stumbling block to me; you do not have in mind the things of God, but the things of men" (Matthew 16:21–23).

Then Jesus called the crowd to Him and taught an important lesson about commitment to the things of God. He said: "If anyone would come after me, he must deny himself and take up his cross and follow me. For whoever wants to save his life will lose it, but whoever loses his life for me and for the gospel will save it. What good is it for a man to gain the whole world, yet forfeit his soul? Or what can a man give in exchange for his soul?" (Mark 8:34–37).

This famous passage lays out the utter seriousness of the commitment to follow God. Jesus was obviously committed to God to the point of giving up His life for all of humanity. He expects nothing less in terms of willingness on the part of His followers. Some have thought that following Jesus' way requires nothing but a vague commitment to knowing something about Him and somehow accepting that He lived and died—believing in Him, in that sense. It is, of course, much more. It involves a commitment to His way of life. It means putting away the self for the sake of others. It means seeking to behave as Christ Himself behaved as a human on this earth.

Jesus then taught about His own second coming and the Judgment. He said, "If anyone is ashamed of me and my words in this adulterous and sinful generation, the Son of Man will be ashamed of him when he comes in his Father's glory with the holy angels" (verse 38).

Looking beyond this life, Jesus began to speak of His own return to the earth. What He said next was a mysterious reference to how He will appear at that time. He said: "I tell you the truth, some who are standing here will not taste death before they see the kingdom of God come with power" (Mark 9:1). It was a prophecy that would be fulfilled about a week later, probably on nearby Mount Hermon, rising over 9,000 feet above sea level. According to the Gospel accounts, Jesus took Peter and the brothers James and John with Him and went up a high mountain. There He began to pray, and as He was doing so, His face shone like the sun and His clothes became as bright as a flash of lightning. Two men appeared and talked to Jesus about His impending death. They were two well-known Old Testament figures, Elijah and Moses.

The disciples were drowsy when this was happening. They came to their senses as the men were leaving. A cloud surrounded them all and a voice was heard confirming the identity of Jesus. The voice said essentially what had been said at Jesus' baptism: "This is my Son, whom I love. Listen to him!" (Mark 9:2–7; Luke 9:28–35).

When the cloud cleared, only Jesus and the disciples remained. Jesus instructed them, "Tell the vision to no one until the Son of Man is risen from the dead" (Matthew 17:6–9, NKJV).

The vision caused the three disciples to ask a question about one of the Old Testament figures they had just seen: "Why is it said that Elijah must come just before the Messiah?" They knew Elijah had died long ago, yet they had just seen him, as if alive, in a vision. It was no doubt very puzzling. Jesus explained that "Elijah" had already come a second time in the form of John the Baptist. In other words, Jesus was showing them yet another indication of who He was. Then, looking toward His own impending death, He also pointed out that ultimate suffering was in His destiny just as it had been for John.

Once down the mountain they found the other disciples surrounded by an argumentative crowd including some teachers of the law. A man had brought his demon-possessed son for healing, but the disciples had been unable to help. The boy was often convulsed and ended up in the fire or in the water.

Jesus rebuked the spirit, which, after shrieking, convulsed the boy for a few moments and left him. The boy looked as pale as a corpse, but Jesus took his hand and lifted him up.

The disciples were puzzled as to why they could not rid the boy of the demon. Jesus said that their faith was lacking and that some demons come out only after prayer and fasting (Mark 9:14–29). In other words, there are some tenacious evil spirits who respond only to those who are especially close to God and fortified by Him.

It was another important lesson for the future when the disciples would not have Jesus physically by their side.

Chapter Six

Reconciling Relationships

Jesus took the opportunity to teach His disciples that a careful process of dispute resolution could heal damaged relationships. Allowing resentments against another to fester only makes matters worse for everyone.

The impending betrayal and death of Jesus Christ was something His disciples could not comprehend, even when Jesus told them directly what was to happen to Him. Why?

The Gospel writer Luke says: "They did not understand what this meant. It was hidden from them, so that they did not grasp it, and they were afraid to ask him about it" (Luke 9:45). There was a point in the time leading up to Jesus' crucifixion when the reality of what was ahead was hidden from His followers. Perhaps this was God's way of preserving the group a little longer.

The conversation about Jesus' death took place along the road from Caesarea Philippi to Capernaum. The disciples had accompanied Jesus to the mountainous north of the country, and three of them had the unusual experience of seeing a vision of their master in the kingdom of God. It was an experience like no other, and it would provide an important anchor for their belief in years to come.

Once the disciples were back in Capernaum, some tax collectors approached Peter and asked whether Jesus paid temple tax. This was no doubt a trap to see whether Jesus was supportive of the religious authorities. Peter told them that Jesus did pay the tax. When Jesus heard about it, He told Peter to go to the nearby lake and throw out a line. He would catch a fish with a coin in its mouth. Then He would be able to pay the collectors the necessary tax (Matthew 17:24–27).

Jesus knew that as the Son of God He was not actually liable for the temple tax, as His conversation with Peter shows. Indeed, Jesus indicated that the disciples were not obliged as subjects of the future kingdom of God to pay temple taxes either. However, He wanted to set an example of obedience to the laws of the land, and so he paid the tax with money provided in a miraculous way.

Like Children, Like Sheep

This period in Jesus' ministry is marked by intensive teaching of His disciples rather than interaction with the crowds. He knew that He had a short time left, perhaps about one year. It was time to educate His immediate followers as fully as He could.

A new opportunity to do so came when they asked a question resulting from a dispute among them. They said, "Who is the greatest in the kingdom of heaven?" They had, in fact, been arguing about which one of them would be the greatest. Their question betrayed a fundamental lack of understanding of what the kingdom of God is all about.

Jesus was able to demonstrate the problem by setting a small child in the midst of them. He said: "I tell you the truth, unless you change and become like little children, you will never enter the kingdom of heaven. Therefore, whoever humbles himself like this child is the greatest in the kingdom of heaven. And whoever welcomes a little child like this in my name welcomes me" (Matthew 18:1–5).

Like so many human beings, the disciples were lost in the striving for power and prestige. They were missing the point that their master was not interested in any of that. His example of the little child was a powerful correction of their self-centered thought processes. They had argued about who would be greatest. Jesus said, "He who is least among you all—he is the greatest" (Luke 9:48). The unexpected key to greatness was humility. It was also a necessity for entry into the kingdom of heaven.

Next, John asked a question about a man who was not with the disciples and yet was doing similar works. John wanted to stop the man from doing his work. Jesus told him to take a more generous approach and not prevent the man from doing good in Jesus' name. Jesus did not say to join the man or to welcome him, just to allow him to do his good work. Again Jesus warned the disciples not to do anything to cause the little ones to sin. Those who did, He said, would be better off being thrown into the sea with a millstone around their neck (Mark 9:38–42).

Jesus also warned against letting any physical desire get in the way of the pursuit of the kingdom of God. Many things cause people to sin, but none should displace the kingdom of God as the preferred goal. He said that it would be better to enter the kingdom physically incapacitated than to fail because of a physical orientation to life (Matthew 18:7–9).

Jesus was also very concerned that the disciples learn the lesson of service to humanity. He asked whether a shepherd does not leave the flock to find a lost sheep. He painted the picture of a loving shepherd whose deep concern for the animals in his care led him to search intensively for one lost out of 99 (verses 12–14). It was a demonstration of God's care for the least of us.

Dispute Resolution

One of the more difficult aspects of human relationships is learning to forgive others. When someone has done something against us, what should we do?

While still in Capernaum, Jesus gave some teaching about this. Not surprisingly, He had to deal with this perennial problem. He said to His disciples, who were as yet unconverted, "If your brother sins against you, go and show him his fault, just between the two of you. If he listens to you, you have won your brother over" (verse 15).

What most people do, of course, is just the opposite. They go to other people and complain about their friend, or relative, or boss. They rarely go to the person who has sinned against them, whether that sin is real or perceived. The result is a poisoning of the atmosphere and a drawing in of others who were not previously involved. Jesus took the opportunity to teach His disciples that a careful process of dispute resolution could heal damaged relationships. Allowing resentments against another to fester only makes matters worse for everyone.

But what are we to do when the person we go to with our complaint doesn't hear us? Jesus said: "But if he will not listen, take one or two others along, so that 'every matter may be established by the testimony of two or three witnesses'" (verse 16).

Calling on the principle in the Old Testament that facts be established before witnesses, Jesus showed that an unresolved private discussion about offenses between two parties has to become more open if reconciliation cannot be effected on the personal level. This requires willingness on both sides for any progress to be made. And if the problem cannot be resolved at this level, then Jesus said, "If he refuses to listen to them, tell it to the church; and if he refuses to listen even to the church, treat him as you would a pagan or a tax collector" (verse 17).

The issue, of course, is a sin against another. If no sin has occurred, then the matter is no cause for debate or offense. If there is a provable sin, and the one who has sinned refuses to hear even a broader group, then the person is to be treated as one who is unconverted.

Reassuring the disciples that His relationship with them was solid and dependable, Jesus added two more thoughts. He said: "I tell you the truth, whatever you bind on earth will be bound in heaven, and whatever you loose on earth will be loosed in heaven. Again, I tell you that if two of you on earth agree about anything you ask for, it will be done for you by my Father in heaven" (verses 18–19). That is to say that the Church, which was to come into formal being in the near future and which the disciples did not yet really comprehend, would be firmly linked to Jesus and His Father. The disciples could be confident that their decisions on behalf of the Church community would be supported, and that even a small group of them assembled before God would have a close relationship with Him.

The issue of forgiveness was obviously still troubling to Peter. He asked: "Lord, how many times shall I forgive my brother when he sins against me? Up to seven times?" Peter wanted to limit the forgiveness we should extend to others when they sin against us. Jesus made it clear that our forgiveness should be limitless. He answered, "I tell you, not seven times, but seventy-seven times" (verses 21–22). Now, this is not to say that where there is an unrepentant attitude, we *can* forgive. In such cases we must have an attitude that is always *willing* to forgive and holds no grudges.

Jesus demonstrated the truth of what He was saying by telling a story about a man who was forgiven a huge debt of millions by his master, and who turned around and had someone else imprisoned for owing an insignificant amount. The result was that the first man was imprisoned by his master and made to pay back the millions. Driving home the point about forgiveness and mercy, Jesus said, "This is how my heavenly Father will treat each of you unless you forgive your brother from your heart" (verses 23–35).

First Priority

Not everyone recognized Jesus for who He was. We have seen that many times already in this study. Even His disciples were only coming to understand after a considerable time with Him.

Not surprisingly, perhaps, His family had the same problem of disbelief. Just before the autumn religious festival known as the Feast of Tabernacles, Jesus' brothers said to Him, "You ought to leave here and go to Judea, so that your disciples may see the miracles you do. No one who wants to become a public figure acts in secret. Since you are doing these things, show yourself to the world." The Gospel writer John adds, "For even his own brothers did not believe in him" (John 7:2–5).

Jesus' reply was that His brothers should go to the Feast, but that He would not go to Jerusalem yet. He knew that this was not the right time for a public appearance. After His brothers had left, He began His journey to the city—but in secret.

On the way He went through Samaria, where previously He had met the woman at the well and declared to her that He was the Christ. Several of her townspeople had also recognized Jesus as the Savior of the world. Now the reception was different. When some messengers went on ahead to prepare for His arrival in a Samaritan village, they were disappointed. The villagers rejected Him because He was going to Jerusalem to worship. The Samaritans claimed that Mount Gerizim in their territory was where God should be worshiped, rather than Jerusalem.

This caused James and John, aptly surnamed the Sons of Thunder by Jesus, to take a vindictive approach. They asked, "Lord, do you want us to call fire down from heaven to destroy them?" (Luke 9:51–54).

Jesus' response was to rebuke His two disciples. He said, "You do not know what manner of spirit you are of. For the Son of Man did not come to destroy men's lives but to save them" (verses 55–56, NKJV).

On the way to another village, a teacher of the law came to Jesus and said that he would follow Him wherever He would go. Jesus pointed out that the cost of discipleship was high, because self-sacrifice and dedication were central (Matthew 8:19–22). He said that "no one who puts his hand to the plow and looks back is fit for service in the kingdom of God" (Luke 9:62).

This was, perhaps, a comment on Christ's own part referencing His forthcoming death. He knew that He had to be single-minded about His immediate purpose.

God With Us?

When Jesus arrived in Jerusalem, the crowds were already asking about Him. He was the subject of considerable debate. Some said He was the Messiah, come at last. Others said He could not be, because the Messiah's origins were unknown, and this man came from Galilee.

In one discussion with them about halfway through the annual weeklong Feast of Tabernacles, Jesus explained to the religious leaders in His audience that He was teaching only what His Father wished. He was not teaching His own ideas. That, He said, is the mark of a man who is God's servant.

Furthermore He said that the religious leaders who were listening were trying to kill Him. The crowd told him He was crazy—demon-possessed—to make such an allegation. But others in the crowd had heard the same thing and concluded that perhaps the authorities thought He truly was the Christ, otherwise they would do something about Him. Some said, "When the Christ comes, will he do more miraculous signs than this man?" (John 7:11–31).

The Pharisees were troubled by this kind of talk. They sent temple guards to arrest Jesus. His response was that He was with them for only a short time, and that He was going to a place where they could not find Him nor go themselves.

It was a puzzle to the crowds. They said, "Where does this man intend to go that we cannot find him? Will he go where our people live scattered among the Greeks, and teach the Greeks? What did he mean when he said, 'You will look for me, but you will not find me,' and 'Where I am, you cannot come'?" (verses 32–36).

On the last day of the Feast, Jesus made a public pronouncement about the coming availability of the Holy Spirit. This was a dramatic new truth. He said, "If anyone is thirsty, let him come to me and drink. Whoever believes in me, as the Scripture has said, streams of living water will flow from within him" (verses 37–38).

What did He mean by this? The writer John says: "By this he meant the Spirit, whom those who believed in him were later to receive. Up to that time the Spirit had not been given, since Jesus had not yet been glorified" (verse 39).

Some people, when they heard these things, concluded that Jesus was the One prophesied by Moses to come. They said, "Surely this man is the Prophet." Others said, "He is the Christ." Still others said that Christ had to come from Bethlehem, yet this man came from Nazareth. They knew nothing of His birth as we do now. So the people were divided over Him. Even the temple guards were confused and did not want to seize Him. The Pharisees said that none of them nor the rulers believed in Him, so why should the crowd? It was a poor argument. Those who did believe did not need the authorities' permission or agreement (verses 40–49).

One of the rulers, however, had met Jesus before. His name was Nicodemus. He said that it would be wise to hear what Jesus had to say before condemning Him out of hand. His colleagues replied with scorn: "Are you from Galilee, too? Look into it, and you will find that a prophet does not come out of Galilee" (verses 50–52).

What was happening is typical of the divide that is caused when some recognize the work that God is doing and others cannot.

Casting Stones

At this point in attempting to harmonize the four Gospel accounts, John's account presents us with a challenge. It contains the story of a woman caught in the act of adultery. It is a section of Scripture that some believe was added later. Though believed to be an authentic account of an actual incident, where it should fit in the chronological record is debated.

Eager to trap Jesus, the scribes and Pharisees brought the adulteress to Him for His judgment. She had been caught in the act—a sin punishable by stoning according to the law of Moses. There are a couple of things to notice about the details of the situation. First, the woman's partner is nowhere to be seen, and second, no witnesses are produced.

With great wisdom Jesus simply started writing in the dust with His finger. The religious leaders kept asking questions. Eventually Jesus straightened up and invited the ones without sin to throw the first stone at the woman. He then returned to writing on the ground. The most senior leaders left first, realizing that Jesus had cornered them. The younger leaders left last, leaving only Jesus and the woman.

Jesus straightened up again and asked the woman, "Where are they? Has no one condemned you?"

She replied, "No one, sir."

"Then neither do I condemn you. Go now and leave your life of sin" (John 8:3–11).

What did He write on the ground? That's been the subject of much speculation, and no one knows. In a sense it is what He said and did that is more important. Jesus showed Himself to be wiser than His enemies, more just and merciful, yet completely supportive of the place of the law of God in human life.

The Shepherd's Voice

During one of His visits to Jerusalem, the Pharisees questioned Jesus about His statement that He is the light of the world. They said that His claim was invalid because He was speaking as His own witness. Jesus pointed out to them that He and His Father were the two witnesses to His claim. He had said that those who followed Him would not walk in darkness but in the light. The Pharisees did not recognize Him, He said, because they did not know the Father. These were strong words to be speaking in the confines of the temple.

Now Jesus again told His audience that He was going to disappear, and that where He was going they could not come. Some thought He meant to kill Himself. Puzzled by His words, they asked Him, "Who are you?" (verse 25). Others, however, put their faith in Him as He spoke.

To those who were less convinced yet still saw something remarkable in Him, Jesus said, "If you hold to my teaching, you are really my disciples. Then you will know the truth, and the truth will set you free" (verses 31–32). Filled with pride, some responded that they were already free and not in slavery to anyone. They claimed to be a special people since they were descended from the patriarchal father, Abraham. Jesus reminded them that they were nevertheless slaves to sin and that He could set them free. He said: "I know you are Abraham's descendants. Yet you are ready to kill me, because you have no room for my word. I am telling you what I have seen in the Father's presence, and you do what you have heard from your father" (verses 37–38).

By this He meant that they were listening to the wrong father. He went on to say that father Abraham was a righteous man and that he would not have sought to kill Jesus. Insultingly they questioned Jesus' origins. They said, "We are not illegitimate"—the implication being that Jesus was, whereas they had God as their father. Even more directly, Jesus then told them that they were of their father the devil, who was a murderer and a liar from the beginning.

Again He drew the distinction for them: "He who belongs to God hears what God says. The reason you do not hear is that you do not belong to God" (verse 47).

The discussion was getting too heated for many of them. Now they replied that He was one of the hated Samaritans, and demon-possessed. When He told them next that He was alive before Abraham, they picked up stones to kill Him, but He was able to avoid them and leave the area of the temple.

A Blind Man Sees

Blindness comes in different forms. It can be physical or spiritual. One is far more serious than the other. In a miraculous show of God's power, Jesus healed a blind man by making mud and placing it on the man's eyes. Then He sent him to the Pool of Siloam to wash. After that, he was able to see.

The man's neighbors had varied reactions. Some said he wasn't the same man who used to beg, while others said he was. The man himself said, "It's me." The Pharisees asked him what had happened, and he told them what Jesus had done. His parents knew that this was their son, but they didn't know how he had come to see. At least, that is what they told the Pharisees who had heard that Jesus had healed the man on the Sabbath.

The Pharisees were spiritually blinded to such a degree that they said of Jesus, "This man is not from God, for he does not keep the Sabbath" (John 9:16). Others disagreed, and so they, too, were divided over Jesus.

When the Pharisees called for the man's parents to explain what had happened, his parents were afraid of being excommunicated. They knew that the Pharisees had threatened to put out of the synagogue anyone who claimed that Jesus was the prophesied Christ. So they said, "Why don't you ask our son to explain? He's old enough to speak for himself" (verse 23, paraphrased).

The Pharisees called for the healed man a second time. Again he was asked to explain. By now he was getting irritated with his questioners. "Why do you want to hear it again? Do you want to become his disciples, too?" he asked (verse 27).

Now the religious leaders got angry. They insulted the man, telling him that he was just a supporter of Jesus and that he was steeped in sin at birth. With that, they threw him out.

When Jesus heard what had happened, He went to the man and comforted him, telling him who He was. The man became a believer.

All of this caused Jesus to remark, "For judgment I have come into this world, so that the blind will see and those who see will become blind" (verse 39).

It was increasingly clear that only certain ones would understand, and that understanding was a gift from the Father. More likely than not, the religious leaders had not been chosen to receive such knowledge at that time. The Pharisees asked if Jesus regarded them as blind. He replied, "If you were blind, you would not be guilty of sin; but now that you claim you can see, your guilt remains" (verse 41). Jesus said that because they claimed they did know and understand, they put themselves in a different category.

Shepherd and Sheep

The whole situation with the healing of the blind man led Jesus to teach another lesson by way of an allegory. He began speaking about a man entering a sheep pen by climbing over the fence. He said such a man is a thief. He said the true shepherd comes in by the gate, and the sheep recognize his voice and follow him. They will not follow a stranger but will rather run away. The audience did not understand this figure of speech, so Jesus explained that He was the gate and also the shepherd. Other teachers were robbers, strangers and hired hands who did not really care for the sheep. When trouble came in the form of a wolf, the hired hands would run away.

Jesus said He was prepared to lay down His life for the sheep. He said that His sheep would recognize His voice. He also said that there were other sheep not of the fold of Israel, alluding to the non-Israelite peoples who would become His followers in future years. He added that He would willingly sacrifice Himself for the sheep—that His Father had allowed Him to do that.

This powerful teaching was too much for some of His Jewish listeners. They said, "He is demon-possessed and raving mad. Why listen to him?" (John 10:20).

As usual, others did not take that approach. They said instead, "These are not the sayings of a man possessed by a demon. Can a demon open the eyes of the blind?" (verse 21).

So it was that Jesus often engendered feelings and opinions that were at opposite ends of the spectrum. His teachings divided people.

Blessed With Understanding

Jesus would send people ahead of Him to prepare the way in the towns and villages He was about to visit. He had done this with His 12 disciples in Galilee; now He commissioned 70 more to go to the area of Perea, which is Jordan today, and into Judea. The men whom He chose would go out in twos to heal the sick and to teach about the kingdom of God. They were not to stay where they were not welcome. They were rather to shake the dust off their feet and go on to the next place.

Saying this, Christ remembered those towns that had rejected Him in Galilee. There was the fishing town of Capernaum, where He had been so much in evidence; the black basalt town of Korazin on the hillside above the Sea of Galilee; and the seashore town of Bethsaida. Jesus said that it would be more tolerable for the gentile cities of Tyre and Sidon in the Day of Judgment than for these cities in His home territory.

When the 70 returned, they were exultant that the demons were subject to them. Christ said that they should rather rejoice in their place in the coming kingdom of God. After all, Jesus said that He had seen Satan, the leader of the demons, fall like lightning from heaven.

The fact that the Father had seen fit to bless these men with such spiritual understanding was a source of great satisfaction to Jesus. He said: "I praise you, Father, Lord of heaven and earth, because you have hidden these things from the wise and learned, and revealed them to little children. Yes, Father, for this was your good pleasure" (Luke 10:21).

Jesus was apparently so pleased about their understanding that He said to them privately, "Blessed are the eyes that see what you see. For I tell you that many prophets and kings wanted to see what you see but did not see it, and to hear what you hear but did not hear it" (verses 23–24).

Two Great Lessons

When a teacher of the law asked Jesus, "What must I do to inherit eternal life?" Jesus had a perfect opportunity to teach a great lesson. He replied with two questions: "What is written in the Law?" and "How do you read it?" (verses 25–26).

The teacher of the law replied: "'Love the Lord your God with all your heart and with all your soul and with all your strength and with all your mind'; and, 'Love your neighbor as yourself.'" Jesus told him that if he would do that, he would live. But the lawyer wanted to go further, so he pursued Jesus with this question: "And who is my neighbor?" (verse 29).

It was the occasion to recount the story of the good Samaritan, who took pity on a robbed and wounded man at the roadside. A shocking aspect of the story was that two others had passed by the man and done nothing. They were both Jews and part of the religious hierarchy. The Jews regarded the Samaritan who stopped and helped as part of a mixed people, religiously and tribally. He would have been considered unclean by the lawyer. The Samaritans, likewise, regarded the Jews as enemies. So Christ was teaching that even our enemy is our neighbor when he needs help. Jesus' message was clear: Be like the Samaritan who showed mercy and was a good neighbor, and you will do well.

Jesus and His disciples came next to Bethany near Jerusalem. There, two sisters, Martha and Mary, welcomed them. Mary was anxious to hear what Jesus had to teach, but Martha was busy with all the preparations for the guests. Martha, upset by her sister's lack of help, complained to Jesus. He explained that there are times to set aside the physical distractions and concentrate on what is spiritually important. That was what Mary had done (verses 38–42).

How to Pray

Just how do we approach God? Is there a special formula? Does God hear and answer only when the formula is followed? Is He really there? How to pray is often a mystery to those who have seldom if ever done it and have never had any instruction.

John the Baptist had taught his disciples to pray. The day now arrived when Jesus' followers requested that He do the same for them.

Jesus' reply to the disciples' request has become immortalized in song and is repeated by rote and often without real meaning in the Western religious tradition— not, of course, what Christ intended. The so-called Lord's Prayer is, in fact, a *pattern* for prayer rather than a prayer to be repeated as a ritual. Let's look closely at Jesus' instruction.

He said, when you pray, say: "Our Father in heaven, hallowed be Your name" (Luke 11:2a, New King James Version throughout the remainder of the chapter). Our approach to God, then, is as to a father. He is to be thought of as a loving father. So many today, however, have not experienced such a relationship with their physical father. That can sometimes get in a person's way. It demonstrates the important effect that a father can have on his child's relationship with God Himself. Now, God can, of course, compensate for such lacks when a person asks Him for help.

The first line of Christ's model prayer goes on to say that God's name is recognized as holy. That is because God is holy. What does this mean? Holiness is a mysterious subject to many. It is the condition of being set apart for a special purpose. God is set apart from us because He is a unique being, both Creator and loving Father of humanity, a being who has always existed. He has created us for a purpose and wants us to fulfill that purpose. We are to approach Him, therefore, with reverence, or respect.

Next, Jesus said we are to acknowledge that God has a kingdom that is to come on the earth, and that we should be looking forward to it. He said that we are to pray: "Your kingdom come. Your will be done on earth as it is in heaven" (verse 2b). Not only are we to anticipate God's kingdom being set up on earth in our prayers, but we are also to look forward to His will being done on the earth as it is done where He dwells in heaven. That is to say that this present world is not where people in general practice God's way; this is not a world that reflects God's ways in action.

The future kingdom of God will be on earth, not in heaven, and as a result human beings will experience God's ways in action everywhere. In today's world we so often wonder where God is when tragedy strikes. We want to blame Him for what has happened, or agonize over why He has not prevented a tragedy. But because most people have opted to seek their own will rather than God's, God is not involved in their day-to-day affairs. In that sense, this is not His world, as Jesus and His followers pointed out. But a time is coming when it will be.

In the following verse we read that we are to seek God's help in providing our daily needs: "Give us day by day our daily bread" (verse 3). In saying this, we acknowledge the source of our well-being. As individuals we recognize that, even though for the time being God stays out of the affairs of humanity as a whole, He still has ultimate control over the physical world He created.

Though human society does not operate according to God's ways, He does provide for His children's needs when they live His way and request His help.

Next, Jesus said we are to pray: "And forgive us our sins, for we also forgive everyone who is indebted to us" (verse 4a). We are to acknowledge that we do commit sins. We are to regularly seek God's forgiveness for our failures to live according to His standards.

What is sin? As we saw earlier, *sin* is an unfashionable word today. The sinner has become a patient in a society dominated by pseudo-psychological explanations of human behavior. People no longer sin, they are victims of their pasts. Too often the excuse is that we had bad experiences as children and cannot be held responsible for our actions. Jesus did not subscribe to that view. He taught that we do sin and that we need to acknowledge it, repent—that is, turn around—and be freed from the guilt that sin causes.

We are also to recognize our need to be willing to forgive others their sins against us and not to hold grudges against them.

Finally, Jesus said that we should pray for protection from the activities of Satan. Jesus understood that there is an archenemy, a powerful spirit who is dedicated to the destruction of humanity.

He taught His disciples to pray with the following principles in mind: "And do not lead us into temptation, but deliver us from the evil one" (verse 4b). It is not that God will put evil in our path so much as it is a statement that we should recognize our need for protection from Satan's destructive intentions toward us.

Keep Knocking

Jesus' instruction about prayer was followed by a lesson in the importance of persistence in prayer. God will answer, but He does not always answer according to our timetable. The human tendency is to give up on prayer because the answer does not come as soon as we want. Boldness or persistence in prayer is expected of us.

In Jesus' example, He told a story of a man wakened at midnight by his friend asking for food for an unexpected visitor. At first the sleepy man was not going to get up and help, but when his friend persisted, he did get up and give him what he needed. So persistence pays off.

Continuing, Jesus showed that God is ready to answer our innermost needs. He said: "Ask, and it will be given to you; seek, and you will find; knock, and it will be opened to you. For everyone who asks receives, and he who seeks finds, and to him who knocks it will be opened" (Luke 11:9–10). The Father is willing to give His Holy Spirit to those who ask Him in sincerity and with a repentant heart. There can be no greater gift. It is the promise of the very mind of God, made available to humans. It is the promise of living forever.

We frail humans know how to give good things to our children. God, our Father, is capable of giving gifts of ultimate value to His children when they ask in honesty and truth.

Chapter Seven

Inside Out

Knowing the hypocrisy of the Pharisees' thought patterns, Jesus took the opportunity to point out to the religious leader that it is what is inside a person that matters, not what is on the outside.

The themes of light and darkness appear more than once in the Bible to denote the reality of God's world and that of Satan. God is real, and so is Satan.

When Jesus brought relief to people caught up in Satan's web of deception, He sometimes faced accusations of being in league with the devil. For example, He drove out a demon from a man who could not say a word. The crowd was amazed when they heard the man speak. Some said that Jesus did such miracles by the power of Beelzebub, the prince of demons. Others were more demanding, asking that He give them some further miraculous sign from heaven. Jesus was prepared to answer both groups.

In response to the charge that He was working under Satan's power, He said that Satan could not be working against himself. It made no sense for Jesus' critics to claim that a person who was working for the devil should free a person who was under Satan's influence. As Jesus said, "A house divided against itself will fall" (Luke 11:17).

He also warned His opponents that they should decide whether or not they were in the presence of God's Spirit at work, and if they were, to be very careful not to judge the work of God as the work of Satan—which, after all, would be blasphemy. Jesus emphasized His point by saying, "He who is not with me is against me, and he who does not gather with me, scatters" (verse 23).

His teaching was so striking to one woman that she called out a blessing on His mother for bringing Him into the world. Jesus' response was that there was something far more important. It was that a blessing comes on those who hear the Word of God and obey it. It is not a matter of who we are but that we hear and obey. This is what counts with God (verses 27–28). So often we are obsessed with the position, status, wealth or fame of a person. God is concerned with innermost intentions—the heart.

It was at this point in speaking to the crowds that Jesus addressed those who had asked for a sign from heaven (verses 29–32). First he commented on the wicked nature of the generation of His time. Then He told them that they would receive no other sign than the sign of Jonah. This was not the first time in His ministry that He had mentioned Jonah as a reference point.

Hundreds of years earlier, the prophet Jonah had brought a warning against the gentile city of Nineveh, and the people there had changed their behavior to such an extent that God had spared their city. Now someone greater than Jonah had come, and the people of Judah were not prepared to listen.

Jesus also mentioned that the queen of Sheba had come to visit King Solomon about a thousand years earlier and had marveled at his wisdom. Yet Jesus' generation had given little attention to Him, the Son of God. It was a pointed condemnation of His own people, because the Ninevites and the queen of Sheba were not Israelites, yet they had recognized God's servants. Jesus' own people were having trouble acknowledging Him.

He went on to encourage His listeners to make sure that they were walking in light, not darkness (verses 33–36). It is all too easy to fall prey to the deceptions of Satan, who is the prince of darkness, the ruler of this present age. We are to seek the light and be focused on truth. If we do that, we will not reject the true light when it is before us, as so many did in Jesus' own time.

Religious Hypocrites I

Setting traps for Jesus was becoming a habit with the Pharisees. While Jesus was an invited guest at dinner with one of them, the Pharisee noted that the young Teacher had not washed His hands in the ritual way.

Knowing the hypocrisy of the Pharisees' thought patterns, Jesus took the opportunity to point out to the religious leader that it is what is inside a person that matters, not what is on the outside. He said, "You Pharisees clean the outside of the cup and dish, but inside you are full of greed and wickedness" (verse 39). They were religious in an outward show, but they had not captured the essence of the law's intent.

Jesus continued, "Woe to you Pharisees, because you give God a tenth of your mint, rue and all other kinds of garden herbs, but you neglect justice and the love of God. You should have practiced the latter without leaving the former undone" (verse 42). They were willing to tithe or pay a tenth of their produce to God, even on the smallest plant or herb, and yet they were not willing to render merciful judgment. Christ said they should tithe; that is part of God's law. But equally they should have rendered judgments with compassion. Their failure to treat fellow human beings with love was not pleasing to God. In the end, such religion counts for little.

Jesus also criticized the Pharisees for their pride in status. He said, "Woe to you Pharisees, because you love the most important seats in the synagogues and greetings in the marketplaces" (verse 43). Their enjoyment recognition and pride of place was too much for the humble Teacher from Galilee.

No doubt we have all met people like that. Yet, while we do not appreciate their vanities, so often we fail to see similar flaws in ourselves.

Jesus' third comment to the Pharisees contained a very bleak image: unmarked and unnoticed graves. He said, "Woe to you, because you are like unmarked graves, which men walk over without knowing it" (verse 44). The Pharisees demanded attention, yet their approach brought them far less. Hypocrisy makes all of us like dead bodies lying in unmarked and unnoticed graves.

Religious Hypocrites II

One of the scribes, or experts in the law, who was listening said that Jesus' strong words insulted his fellow lawyers.

Now Jesus replied with a powerful series of criticisms of this group (verses 46–52). He said that they weighed people down with their overly strict interpretation of the law and then would not lift a finger to help the burdened. He said they were the same as their forefathers, who had killed God's own prophets. He told them that they would be held responsible for the killing of those messengers. There is also a warning here for us, that we do not reject the Word of God when it is set before us.

Jesus' final words were left to ring in the scribe's ears. He said, "Woe to you experts in the law, because you have taken away the key to knowledge. You yourselves have not entered, and you have hindered those who were entering" (verse 52).

The experts in the Word of God had actually deprived the people of the key to knowledge of God. This was their most serious failing. The very subject that they were supposed to teach, they had failed to deliver. The most important part of their role was to help people understand the Word of God, and they had thrown away the key.

Jesus' open rebuke of the scribes and Pharisees provoked heightened hostility. Now they began to besiege Jesus with trick questions to entrap Him.

This antagonistic encounter caused Jesus to warn the crowds of the hypocrisy of the Pharisees (Luke 12:1–3). He said that there is nothing concealed that will not be revealed. Whatever we do will eventually come to light. If it is evil, it cannot be covered up. It is a realization that has stopped some people short. Knowing that we will be judged on what we have said and done is a powerful motivation to repent and do the right things in life.

Fear God, Not Man

As Jesus went on to say, we should not fear those who can kill the physical body, but rather God who is in charge of our ultimate destiny. He has the power to destroy forever those who will not repent. They will simply never live up to the potential that God desires for all. God does not forget anyone; His care for us is immense (verses 4–7). However, He cannot work with those who willfully reject Him.

Jesus told His listeners that those who were more afraid of man than of God would not succeed. He was God's Son, and His followers should not be afraid of men. If they were willing to disown Him before men, then they would be disowned before the angels of God. Jesus also warned them, as He had before, that speaking against the Holy Spirit of God was blasphemy, a sin that cannot be forgiven, because it is a denial of the power of God (verses 8–10).

Indeed it was the Holy Spirit that would help them know what to say when they would stand accused before the religious authorities. That was their reason not to fear or to fall prey to the temptation to deny Jesus Christ.

The day was coming when His followers would find themselves in such circumstances.

True Riches

As Jesus was addressing a large crowd, probably in Judea, someone called out a request. A man said, "Teacher, tell my brother to divide the inheritance with me" (verse 13).

The question allowed Jesus to instruct about the perils of pursuing the false god of materialism. He told the man that He was not a judge of such matters. Instead, in reply, he focused on avoiding greed. He said, "A man's life does not consist in the abundance of his possessions" (verse 15).

Then He told a story about a rich man whose land was so productive that he had to build new storage places for his wealth. Impressed with his abundance, he told himself that he could now sit back and eat, drink and be merry. But that night God required of him his life, and the rich man was unable to say who would inherit the wealth that he had planned to enjoy himself. God named him a fool for his selfishness. Jesus' conclusion was that "this is how it will be with anyone who stores up things for himself but is not rich toward God" (verse 21).

Now the disciples were about to hear something they had heard before in the Sermon on the Mount. Their Master went on to say that they should not be overly anxious about what to eat or what to wear. God takes care of the birds of the air. They do not starve. He clothes the lilies of the field. They are in fact dressed better than one of Israel's most wealthy kings, Solomon. We humans cannot add a single hour to our lives by worrying. We must learn that God will take care of all these physical matters. The priority, Jesus said, is to seek the Father's kingdom, and then all these other physical needs will be taken care of. It is a question of where our priorities lie, because where our treasure is, there will our hearts be (verse 34).

Readying for Christ's Return

It was not only against materialism that Jesus warned. He also said that we should not be negligent about the time of His return (verses 35–40). Materialism can, of course, make the possibility of His second coming seem very distant. Why worry about it now? Surely there will be a time later, people say.

He said that we should be like servants waiting for their master to return from a wedding banquet. If he finds them watching for his return, he will come in and serve them a meal. Jesus made the point that He will come at a time when He is not expected. So we must be personally diligent if we want to be part of those favored at that time.

Peter asked whether Jesus was giving this warning to the crowd or to the disciples. Jesus replied in a way that signaled that the disciples were to be the primary recipients of His words. He said that a good servant would be providing good food to the household that was left in his charge. He would not be found beating the household, abusing his charges (verses 41–46).

In this way Jesus was warning that those who would be His followers should care for His people, not take advantage of them. Sadly, this is the way some people behave when they think that Jesus' return may be far off. No need to worry about that now, they say.

Jesus concluded His warning this way: "That servant who knows his master's will and does not get ready or does not do what his master wants will be beaten with many blows. But the one who does not know and does things deserving punishment will be beaten with few blows. From everyone who has been given much, much will be demanded; and from the one who has been entrusted with much, much more will be asked" (verses 47–48).

The lesson is clear: We are responsible for acting on what we know and for carrying out our responsibilities in a godly way. The disciples were to become teachers themselves, responsible for serving God's people and for telling them the truth. They had no excuse not to do so.

Of Division and Discernment

Jesus concluded His address to the crowds with two more warnings—one about coming division, and the other about right judgment.

He said that He had come to eventually render judgment on the earth, but that would come after He had first died a sacrificial death. "Do you think I came to bring peace on earth? No, I tell you, but division" (verse 51).

It was a shocking statement, and not one we prefer to think about. It sounds unlike the stereotypical gentle Teacher from Nazareth. And it is. But Jesus Christ did not always smooth things over. Sometimes following the Father's way means that there will be separation, even within families. It is inevitable that in a world of compromises with evil, those who stand for truth, and practice it, will be divided from those who do not.

Jesus' final warning was to those who refused to discern the times. He told His audience that they could predict weather conditions by looking at the sky or gauging wind directions. What they seemed unable to do was to exercise discernment about the turbulent conditions that surrounded them.

They simply would not do the right thing, and they were going to suffer as a result.

Time for Change

Do we assume that when tragedy befalls a person, he or she must have sinned in some extraordinary way?

Jesus addressed this idea when some said they had witnessed the brutal death of some of their fellow countrymen. Apparently the Roman governor of Judea, Pontius Pilate, had killed certain Galileans while they were sacrificing at the temple. He had then mixed their blood with that of their offerings—an act of great desecration. Jesus asked the crowd whether they thought these poor victims had suffered so because they were guilty of worse sins than other people.

While His answer was no, they were not worse sinners, He took the opportunity to point out that all sin must be repented of. If we do not repent and change our ways, He said, we will all perish, whether by the hand of a military ruler or otherwise.

Jesus added to His argument by asking about another specific case of tragedy with which His audience was familiar. He said, "Those eighteen who died when the tower in Siloam fell on them—do you think they were more guilty than all the others living in Jerusalem?" (Luke 13:4). The answer was again no. But the point He made was that all of us will die forever if we do not repent of our sins.

Emphasizing that sometimes God allows a certain period for repentance, Jesus told a parable (verses 6–9) about a fig tree that did not bear fruit over a three-year period— understood to be a reference to the length of His ministry to that point and to His rejection by His own people. He said that at the end of three years the owner of the fig tree ordered that the tree be cut down. His laborer asked for a little more time for the tree; if after fertilizing it did not bear fruit in the next year, it should be destroyed. This is thought to refer to the possibility of fruit being borne from Jesus' work among His own people within the last few months of His life. That would have been in the fourth year of His ministry. Certainly the principle is that, while time is given for repentance, God's mercy does not extend forever. The time comes when He says enough is enough.

Untying Humanity

One of the issues that had arisen during Jesus' ministry was that of correct Sabbath observance. Jesus had made it clear that He was willing to do good deeds on the Sabbath. And He said the Sabbath was made for man, not man for the Sabbath. When He healed a woman who had been crippled for 18 years, the ruler of the local synagogue rebuked the people for asking for healing on the Sabbath. He said, "There are six days for work. So come and be healed on those days, and not on the Sabbath" (verse 14).

Jesus' response was to show the hypocrisy of such a statement. He said that His critics would willingly untie an ox or a donkey on the Sabbath and lead it out to water; why, then, should he not "untie" a woman with an affliction? This was a humiliating example for the synagogue ruler, but the people were pleased with Jesus' reply.

Jesus went on to explain in a couple of examples the nature of the kingdom of God. He said it is like a mustard seed, one of the smallest of seeds, capable of growing to a substantial size. It is also like yeast, which spreads throughout a lump of dough (verses 18–21). In other words, the kingdom of God, which is yet to come in its fullness on the earth, will grow from a small beginning now in the lives of the few into global dominance. It will spread throughout the earth.

That is the future of this war-weary world. There is a time yet ahead when all of humanity will at last live under ideal conditions. That is the message of the kingdom of God that Jesus Christ brought. As we hear each day's news headlines, we see the desperate plight of the world's peoples, and we know the answer must come from beyond us. That is what the Bible teaches. God will intervene to save us from ourselves.

Jesus' Real Identity

During the next winter Jesus went to the temple at the time of the Feast of Dedication, known today as the Festival of Lights, or Hanukkah. Though not a biblically commanded celebration, it commemorates the deliverance of the Jewish people in 164 B.C.E. from the bloody conqueror Antiochus Epiphanes, king of Syria. The Gospel of John provides the only mention of the festival in the Bible.

As Jesus walked in the outer colonnaded area of the temple, a number of Jerusalemites gathered around Him and asked about His identity. They said, "How long will you keep us in suspense? If you are the Christ, tell us plainly" (John 10:24).

Jesus reminded them that He had told them before, but they had not believed Him. He said that His works proved who He was and that His followers heard in Him the voice of the Shepherd. God had given those followers the ability to recognize His Son, and they could not be snatched away from their relationship with the Father. Jesus also made a third statement regarding His identity, saying that He and the Father had a unity of spirit and approach. He explained, "I and the Father are one" (verse 30).

This was a red rag to His Jewish listeners. They claimed falsely that He had committed blasphemy by equating Himself with God the Father. As a result, they picked up stones and were ready to kill Him.

Jesus' response was to quote part of a psalm to them in which the Hebrew word for "gods," *elohim*, is used. He said, "Is it not written in your Law, 'I have said you are gods'?" (verse 34). In Hebrew *elohim* can also mean "judges." In a play on words, Jesus was saying that if God could apply that word to humans, meaning "judges," how much more could He apply it to His own Son, who is part of the God family, and mean "god"? Once again Jesus was telling them who He really was.

Further, He said that they should not believe Him if He did not do the works of the Father. But if they could recognize that such works were being done, then they should accept them as physical proof of what God was doing through Him.

This argument made very little impression, except to convince them to try to take Him into custody. But Jesus eluded them and went on His way across the Jordan to the area known as Perea, where John the Baptist had first baptized people.

What John had taught about Jesus now had its effect. The people in Perea commented, "All that John said about this man was true" (verse 41). As a result, many people believed in Jesus.

Two Ways of Living

Making a tour of various towns and villages, Jesus traveled slowly back in the direction of Jerusalem. On the way someone asked whether only a few people are going to be saved. Jesus' answer cut to the heart of the problem with human nature. He said that we should "make every effort to enter through the narrow door, because many . . . will try to enter and will not be able to" (Luke 13:24).

At the time of the judgment there will be those who will claim that they have worked in Jesus Christ's name, and He will tell them that He does not recognize them. They will argue, "[but] we ate and drank with you, and you taught in our streets." He will say to them, "I don't know you or where you come from. Away from me, all you evildoers!" (verses 26–27).

It was a powerful warning to any who would be complacent about their familiarity with Jesus, then and now. It is not a matter of knowledge but of doing what He says. Head knowledge is of little consequence if it is not practiced.

Jesus completed His answer with a startling image for the self-satisfied. He said, "There will be weeping there, and gnashing of teeth, when you see Abraham, Isaac and Jacob and all the prophets in the kingdom of God, but you yourselves thrown out. People will come from east and west and north and south, and will take their places at the feast in the kingdom of God. Indeed there are those who are last who will be first, and first who will be last" (verses 28–30). We all need to guard against the temptation to sit back and assume that we will be on the right side at that time. It is not our *claim* to be following God but our actual practice of "the narrow way" that matters.

Now some of the Pharisees approached Jesus and advised Him to leave Perea because, they said, "Herod wants to kill you." Perea was in the territory of Herod Antipas.

Jesus replied with as strong a reply about a political leader as you will find in the Gospels. He said, "Go, tell that fox, 'Behold, I cast out demons and perform cures today and tomorrow, and the third day I shall be perfected.' Nevertheless I must journey today, tomorrow, and the day following; for it cannot be that a prophet should perish outside of Jerusalem" (verses 32–33, NKJV).

Jesus recognized the cunning of Herod, who had, after all, been responsible for the imprisonment and death of John the Baptist. He also knew that His own ministry was coming to an end. When He spoke of healing today and tomorrow, and the third day being perfected, He meant that He would reach His goal in a short time. There was still work to do, but it was almost over. And it was in Jerusalem, not Perea, that He would finally be rejected.

Jesus concluded with a heartfelt expression of concern for the city of Jerusalem and all that had happened to those who had come there on God's authority. He said, "O Jerusalem, Jerusalem, you who kill the prophets and stone those sent to you, how often I have longed to gather your children together, as a hen gathers her chicks under her wings, but you were not willing! Look, your house is left to you desolate. I tell you, you will not see me again until you say, 'Blessed is he who comes in the name of the Lord'" (verses 34–35).

In part it was a prophetic statement of the desolation that would come at the hands of the Roman military in 70 C.E. The destruction of the city would result from the rejection of Jesus as the One who could have prevented such a tragedy. It was also no doubt a reference to the many years since then, in which Jesus has not been a part of the life of the majority of His own ethnic group. After His death, He said, the people of Jerusalem would not see Him again until the day of His return to the earth.

Three Parables

Later, on a Sabbath day, Jesus was at a meal with a prominent Pharisee. The usual careful watch was being kept to see whether the young rabbi would somehow break one of the strict rules of the religious group.

In front of Jesus was a man with a medical condition. Perceiving the hypocrisy of His hosts, Jesus asked the Pharisees and the legal experts present whether it was lawful to heal on the Sabbath. Interestingly, none of the experts answered Him. So He went ahead and healed the man. He then asked whether they would pull their own ox out of a well on the Sabbath. Obviously they would, but again they said nothing.

Noting that He was in the presence of people who were filled with pride of position and status, He took the opportunity to teach some lessons in humility, impartiality and dedication. He did this by relating three parables.

Humility is hard to find in today's world. The world of the scribes and Pharisees was really no different. They enjoyed the social prominence that their status gave them. But Jesus said that when they were invited to a wedding feast they should take the lowest or least distinguished seat at the table. That way their host could always elevate them if he wished. Otherwise, if they had taken the seat of honor without being invited to do so, they risked the humiliation of being asked to take a lower seat. He concluded, "For everyone who exalts himself will be humbled, and he who humbles himself will be exalted" (Luke 14:11).

Turning to His host, Jesus said, "When you give a luncheon or dinner, do not invite your friends, your brothers or relatives, or your rich neighbors; if you do, they may invite you back and so you will be repaid." The need to practice impartiality was Jesus' point. He went on, "But when you give a banquet, invite the poor, the crippled, the lame, and the blind, and you will be blessed. Although they cannot repay you, you will be repaid at the resurrection of the righteous" (verses 12–14).

Some at the table with Him commented on the blessing it will be to attend such a meal in the kingdom of God. In reply, Jesus told a pointed story about a man who prepared a great feast for many people (verses 16–24). The guests were told that the meal was ready, and they began to make all kinds of excuses for not being able to come. One said that he had just purchased some land and needed to see it. Another said that he had bought some oxen and needed to try them out. A third said he was just married and could not make it.

The servant of the man who was giving the banquet returned and told his master, who became angry and ordered his servant to open the banquet to the disadvantaged and anyone else who could come. But the servant was to keep out those originally invited. Their ingratitude had prevented them from sharing the feast.

The lesson was obvious. The religious leaders, who did not recognize Jesus for who He was, would be shut out of the kingdom of God.

These three parables reinforce three important principles in life. We need an abundance of humility, we need to be fair toward all people, and we must not reject the offer of a place in the kingdom of God by making excuses after we are invited to participate.

Counting the Cost

Jesus' travels in Perea were almost at an end. Soon He would have to go to Jerusalem and face death. In this context He repeated that the cost of discipleship was high. He said that anyone who was not prepared to carry his own cross and follow Him was not worthy of being a disciple.

He advised that people should count the cost before committing to a course of action. Builders should not build buildings without cost estimates and the financial backing to complete the work. Similarly, leaders do not go to war unless they believe they can win and are committed to doing so (Luke 14:28–33). A willingness to give all may be necessary to achieve the goal at hand. As Jesus pointed out, followers must not be bland people, like salt that has lost its flavor (verses 34–35). There must be inner strength. No one will achieve much as a disciple of Christ without wholehearted commitment.

Chapter Eight

The Repentant and the Self-Righteous

We can see from these three examples of things lost—the sheep, the coin and the son—that God the Father is always ready to forgive and restore when we repent and change our ways.

One day Jesus was surrounded by tax collectors and sinners. They were genuinely listening to what He had to say, unlike the pious scribes and Pharisees nearby, who were muttering to themselves about Jesus even talking to such people.

It was an appropriate time for Jesus to point out that His work was to speak with those who needed His spiritual help, not those who thought they did not. So He told three stories to make His point. The stories have certain common elements: all concern something that has been lost and is now found, and over which there is rejoicing as a result; and all focus on a deep change of heart, a repentance that is meaningful.

The first parable was about seeking out a lost sheep. Shepherds will leave 99 safe sheep and go out after one that is lost. This was Jesus' analogy of what He does when He seeks out the one person who needs His help. He is willing to work very hard for the person in trouble to bring him or her to wholeness. When that one lost sheep is found, there is much happiness. In this way Jesus, telling the story with the religious leaders present, justified His approach to humanity. His conclusion was, "I say to you that likewise there will be more joy in heaven over one sinner who repents than over ninety-nine just persons who need no repentance" (Luke 15:7, NKJV).

Next He spoke about a woman who lost one of 10 silver coins. She looked diligently until she found it. When it was found, she was so happy that she invited her neighbors over to celebrate. Making the same point as before, Jesus said, "Likewise, I say to you, there is joy in the presence of the angels of God over one sinner who repents" (verse 10, NKJV).

The third story is a more complex one, but the point is the same. A wise man had two sons, one of whom asked for his inheritance early. The father gave it, and the son squandered it on wild living. He hit rock bottom when finally he had nothing left and took a job looking after pigs. He was so hungry that he even considered eating the pigs' food. The young man came to his senses and realized that he should go home repentant and ask for his father's forgiveness. He said to himself, "I will set out and go back to my father and say to him: Father, I have sinned against heaven and against you. I am no longer worthy to be called your son; make me like one of your hired men" (verses 18–19).

In this parable the son is clearly repentant. This is a model of how we in a repentant spirit should approach our heavenly Father.

In the story, while the son was still a long way off, the father saw him coming. He was filled with compassion for him, ran to his son, threw his arms around him and kissed him. The son apologized to his father. The father's response was to bring the best clothes and put a ring on his finger and sandals on his feet. That night there was a banquet in the son's honor. The father was celebrating what had been lost and was now found.

We can see from these three examples of things lost— the sheep, the coin and the son—that God the Father is always ready to forgive and restore when we repent and change our ways.

In an effort to bring the lesson home to the scribes and the Pharisees, Jesus added an account of the older brother's reaction to the return of the repentant son. He was jealous and angry and refused to go in to the banquet. He was unwilling to accept his brother's repentant return. His father said to him, "My son, you are always with me, and everything I have is yours. But we had to celebrate and be glad, because this brother of yours was dead and is alive again; he was lost and is found" (verses 31–32).

Like the resentful elder brother, the scribes and the Pharisees were not willing that the tax collectors and sinners who surrounded Jesus should repent. In these three stories Jesus drew a striking contrast between repentant sinners and self-righteous hypocrites.

Money Matters

This story of the young man who wasted all of his inheritance, known popularly as the Prodigal Son, led Jesus into more teaching about the right use of money. He said: "There was a certain rich man who had a steward, and an accusation was brought to him that this man was wasting his goods. So he called him and said to him, 'What is this I hear about you? Give an account of your stewardship, for you can no longer be steward'" (Luke 16:1–2, NKJV).

This caused the steward, or manager, to worry about his own financial future. He shrewdly decided to call on his master's debtors and negotiate a reduction in what they owed. When the payments came in, the master commended the wily manager, because his self-interest had produced a good result. Jesus said: "The people of this world are more shrewd in dealing with their own kind than are the people of the light" (verse 8). He was commending the wise use of material possessions to provide for the future, not the underlying craftiness of the steward. Money can be used as a blessing for others. Jesus said: "Use worldly wealth to gain friends for yourselves, so that when it is gone, you will be welcomed into eternal dwellings" (verse 9). There is a wise and godly use of money. It can be used to teach about the kingdom of God, so that when the day comes when such currency is no longer the medium of exchange, it will have been put to good use.

Jesus went on to explain something else about material possessions. People who prove that they can be trusted with a little can also be trusted with much. In the same way, whoever is dishonest with very little will be dishonest with much. If we can't be trusted in dealing with this world's wealth, how can we be trusted with true spiritual riches?

Jesus emphasized that we cannot serve two masters. We have to get physical wealth into perspective. It is not the most important thing in the world. As Jesus said, you cannot serve both God and money.

Some of the Pharisees, who were lovers of money, sneered when they heard this. Jesus said to them, "God knows your hearts" (verse 15). He explained that their wealth should not be thought of as a blessing for their keeping the law, because in fact they did not keep the law properly.

Giving an example from the society of the time, Jesus said, "Whoever divorces his wife and marries another commits adultery; and whoever marries her who is divorced from her husband commits adultery" (verse 18, NKJV). His point was that the Pharisees were not to misapply the law, including the portion governing marriage.

He continued with a story about a rich man who dressed well and ate well every day. Outside his gate sat a beggar named Lazarus, who longed just to eat whatever fell from the rich man's table. Eventually the beggar died, and in the parable angels carried him away to be with Abraham. The rich man also died and was buried. Pictured in torment, and seeing Abraham and Lazarus far off, the rich man begged for their help. Abraham's reply was "Son, remember that in your lifetime you received your good things, and likewise Lazarus evil things; but now he is comforted and you are tormented. And besides all this, between us and you there is a great gulf fixed, so that those who want to pass from here to you cannot, nor can those from there pass to us" (verses 25–26, NKJV).

The rich man then begged Abraham to send Lazarus to his brothers to warn them of what had happened to him. Abraham said, "Let them rather listen to Moses and the prophets to gain understanding about the right use of wealth." The rich man replied, "But if someone from the dead goes to them they will repent." Abraham said, "If they will not listen to Moses and the prophets, someone returning from the dead will not convince them" (verses 29–31, paraphrased).

In these examples about the right use of riches, Jesus taught that we should use money wisely and also with compassion for the less fortunate.

Four Reminders

Jesus would often teach His disciples privately about what they should do after He was no longer with them. On one occasion He rehearsed four important principles about sin, forgiveness, faith and the need to do more than is required.

First He said, "Things that cause people to sin are bound to come, but woe to that person through whom they come" (Luke 17:1). He said it would be better to have a heavy stone hung around our neck and be thrown into the sea than to cause offense to one of His people by our sins.

Next He gave advice about a brother who sins. He said we should point it out and forgive if our brother changes. We are to forgive as many times in a day as our brother repents. There is no limit on forgiveness in this sense.

Knowing their own weaknesses, the disciples then asked Jesus to increase their faith. He replied, "If you have faith as a mustard seed, you can say to this mulberry tree, 'Be pulled up by the roots and be planted in the sea,' and it would obey you" (verse 6, NKJV)—the point being that even a tiny amount of true faith can accomplish the miraculous.

Finally, Jesus related a parable to teach the principle of going over and above what is expected of us. He said that a man does not thank his employee for doing what he has been hired to do. So our approach to following His way of life should be to say, "We are unworthy servants; we have only done our duty" (verse 10). By this He meant that we should go over and above and beyond what is expected of us in doing what is right.

Raising the Dead

One day Jesus heard news that His friend Lazarus was very ill. Lazarus was the brother of two of Jesus' followers, Mary and Martha. Despite hearing of His friend's serious illness, however, Jesus waited two more days before going back to Judea.

His disciples tried to warn Him of the danger of going to a place where the Jews had recently tried to stone Him. Jesus' response was that He could not be deterred by danger, and He knew that Lazarus's illness was for a great purpose. Jesus told His disciples, "Lazarus is dead," preparing them for the miracle that was about to take place.

When He arrived in Bethany, about two miles from Jerusalem, He found that Lazarus had been in his tomb for four days.

The dead man's sister Martha came out to meet Jesus and said, "If you had been here, my brother would not have died" (John 11:21).

Jesus replied, "Your brother will rise again."

Martha responded that she knew he would be in the resurrection at the last day. Jesus then taught her that He is closely connected with the resurrection and eternal life. He said, "He who believes in me will live, even though he dies" (verse 25).

Martha said she understood and believed that, and went back and called her sister, Mary, telling her, "The Teacher is here and is asking for you." Mary got up quickly and left the house, along with those who were comforting her.

Jesus was moved when He saw the depth of their sorrow and asked where Lazarus's body was laid. Now Jesus Himself was weeping. There has been speculation as to why Jesus wept, since He knew He was about to perform a miracle and raise Lazarus from the dead. Some have suggested that rather than sorrow over his death, it was sorrow tinged with anger at their lack of faith. Some of them said, "Could not he who opened the eyes of the blind man have kept this man from dying?" (verse 37).

Jesus now came to the tomb, which was a cave with a stone across the entrance. "Take away the stone," He said.

Martha protested, "But, Lord, by this time there is a bad odor, for he has been there four days" (verse 39).

They took away the stone and Jesus prayed for the benefit of the people standing there, so that they could have faith in Him and believe that God had sent Him. Then He said in a loud voice, "Lazarus, come out!" (verse 43).

The dead man came out with his hands and feet wrapped with linen and a cloth around his face—typical of the way people were buried in those days. Some of the people who saw what Jesus did were convinced of His Messiahship. Others went to the Pharisees and told them what had happened.

The chief priests and the Pharisees called a meeting of their council, the Sanhedrin. They said, "What are we accomplishing? Here is this man performing many miraculous signs. If we let Him go on like this, everyone will believe in Him, and then the Romans will come and take away both our place and our nation" (verses 47–48).

The high priest, Caiaphas, then prophesied that Jesus would die for the Jewish people and for the world. The other religious leaders obviously took the high priest seriously, because as John's Gospel says, "from that day on they plotted to take his life" (verse 53).

Aware of this, Jesus no longer moved publicly among the Jews. He went instead to a place near the Jordan valley, called Ephraim, and stayed there for a while with His disciples. Soon He would begin the last journey of His life to Jerusalem.

False Messiahs

Before Jesus returned to Jerusalem, He traveled a circuitous route through northern Samaria into Galilee and then turned south into the Jordan Valley and Perea. He did this perhaps to avoid the general public before arriving in the capital.

In one Galilean village along the way, He met 10 men with leprosy who begged Him to heal them. He told them to go and show themselves to the priests, and as they went, they were all miraculously healed. Yet only one of them, a Samaritan, turned back and thanked Him. Jesus asked where the other nine were, remarking that it was a non-Jew who had returned and thanked God (Luke 17:11–19). As was often the case, Jesus was recognized as the Son of God by the most unlikely and marginalized in society.

In the Gospel of Luke we are reminded again that the kingdom of God was among the people at that time, yet it seems that many of the Jews did not have eyes to see. Jesus told His disciples that the time was coming when they would wish to see one of the days when He was on the earth, but it would not be possible.

He also warned them against running after false messiahs. He said that His subsequent return to the earth would be like lightning flashing and lighting up the sky from one end to the other. But He said that He must first suffer many things and be rejected by His own generation.

Speaking of social conditions just before His second coming, He compared the times to the days of Noah, just before the Flood, and the days of Lot, just before the destruction of Sodom and Gomorrah. He said, "It will be just like this on the day the Son of Man is revealed" (verse 30). In both cases the majority were unprepared for catastrophe. They went on with daily life oblivious to the fact that destruction was looming.

Jesus said that when He returns, His followers should be ready to flee and not go back into their homes for anything. He said that whoever tries to keep his life in that circumstance will lose it, and whoever loses his life will preserve it.

Of Persistence and Pride

Jesus went on to give a parable to make a different point—the need for persistence in prayer.

He told the story of a widow who persisted in asking a judge to help against her adversary. The judge refused for quite a while, but because she did not give up trying, eventually he said, "I will see that she gets justice, so that she won't . . . wear me out with her [persistence]" (Luke 18:1–5).

Jesus observed that if an unjust judge responds because of persistence, how much more will the *just* judge—God—respond with justice for His people when they are persistent in their prayers to Him.

Noting the human proclivity to lack such faithful persistence, Jesus posed a rhetorical question in conclusion. He asked, "When the Son of Man comes, will he find faith on the earth?" (verse 8).

To try to help some around Him who were self-righteous, Jesus told another parable about prayer. He said that two men went up to the temple to pray, one a Pharisee and the other a tax collector.

The Pharisee stood and proudly prayed, "God, I thank you that I am not like other men—robbers, evildoers, adulterers—or even like this tax collector. I fast twice a week and give a tenth of all I get."

Jesus contrasted the disdainful attitude of the Pharisee with that of the tax collector, who wouldn't even look up to heaven but said, "God, have mercy on me, a sinner." Jesus said it was the tax collector who went home cleansed before God. The Pharisee's self-exaltation had stood in his own way (verses 9–14).

Of Marriage and Children

When Jesus had finished these parables, He left Galilee and went to the other side of the Jordan. Once again crowds of people came to Him, including some Pharisees.

They tested Him by asking, "Is it lawful for a man to divorce his wife?" (Mark 10:2). They knew what Jesus taught about God's original intention for marriage—that it should not be dissolved. They also knew that Moses had permitted divorce under certain circumstances. In raising the subject, perhaps Jesus' enemies thought that they had caught Him teaching things contrary to Moses.

In reply to their question, Jesus asked them, "What did Moses command you?" They said, "Moses permitted a man to write a certificate of divorce and send her away" (verses 3–4). Jesus' reply was that Moses only gave this allowance because of the hardness of their hearts. He explained that from the beginning God intended a man and his wife to be united as one flesh for life. "Therefore," He said, "what God has joined together, let man not separate" (verse 9).

Later, when they were in a house, the disciples asked Jesus to clarify. So He said to them, "Anyone who divorces his wife and marries another woman commits adultery against her. And if she divorces her husband and marries another man, she commits adultery" (verses 10–12). The disciples commented that if it is supposed to be that way in marriage, it is better not to be married. In other words, marriage is a very serious long-term commitment, and too difficult for many. Jesus agreed, saying that those who could accept His teaching should (Matthew 19:10–12).

At this point young children were brought to Jesus so that He could bless them. But His disciples rebuked the people for doing so. This made Jesus indignant. He said, "Let the little children come to Me, and do not forbid them; for of such is the kingdom of God. Assuredly, I say to you, whoever does not receive the kingdom of God as a little child will by no means enter it" (Mark 10:13–15, NKJV).

The disciples still had a lot to learn about their Master and about humility.

Lessons in Living Forever

When a young ruler came to Jesus and asked Him, "Good teacher, what must I do to inherit eternal life?" He reminded him that only God is good and that he must obey the commandments (Luke 18:18–19; Matthew 19:16–17).

"Which ones?" the man inquired.

Jesus began by listing five of the Ten Commandments. He focused on the ones dealing with loving our neighbor as ourselves. The young man said that he had done such things since he was a child. Jesus said, "If you want to be perfect, go, sell your possessions and give to the poor, and you will have treasure in heaven. Then come, follow me" (Matthew 19:18–21). This was too much for the young man, because he had great wealth. He had his limits.

Jesus told His disciples that it is very hard for a rich man to enter the kingdom of heaven. In fact, He said, it is easier for a camel to go through the eye of a needle. This amazed His disciples, and they said, "Who then can be saved?" (verses 23–25). Obviously they thought that the privileges of the wealthy extend to the kingdom of God. Of course, they do not. But as Christ said, despite this, even a rich man can enter the kingdom of God, because with God all things are possible.

Peter recognized that he and the other disciples had done the right thing. He said, "We have left everything to follow you." Jesus told them that, as a result, in the kingdom of God they would sit on 12 thrones judging the 12 tribes of Israel. Indeed, everyone who has given up possessions or family for Christ's sake will inherit eternal life and be rewarded. In this way those who are least privileged in this life will have the opportunity to come first, and those who are most privileged may come last.

In teaching the same principle, Jesus told a parable concerning a landowner who went out early in the morning to hire men to work in his vineyard. He said this was a word picture to teach something about the kingdom of God. The landowner agreed to pay the workers a certain amount for the day. Later in the day he went out and hired more men, saying, "I will pay you whatever is right." Twice more in the day he did the same thing (Matthew 20:1–5).

Toward the end of the day he hired even more men, and when the evening came he said to his foreman, "Call the workers and pay them their wages, beginning with the last ones hired and going on to the first" (verses 6–8).

Those who had worked only about an hour were given the same as the landowner had agreed to pay those hired first. Thinking that they had somehow been cheated, those hired first began to grumble against the landowner.

The landowner replied, "I am not being unfair to you. Didn't you agree to work for a denarius? Take your pay and go. I want to give the man who was hired last the same as I gave you. Don't I have the right to do what I want with my own money? Or are you envious because I am generous?" (verses 13–15).

This was another way of teaching that in God's way of doing things, the last may be first and the first last. It is not a matter of privilege or status or tenure with God. It is a matter of His choosing.

A Lesson in Humility

As noted earlier, Jesus had begun His final journey to Jerusalem. Apparently this was quite a surprise to His disciples, because they knew that there had been a recent attempt to stone Him in the city. So He took them aside and said, "We are going up to Jerusalem, and the Son of Man will be betrayed to the chief priests and the teachers [experts] of the law. They will condemn him to death and will turn him over to the Gentiles to be mocked and flogged and crucified. On the third day he will be raised to life!" (verses 17–19).

Luke's Gospel tells us that the disciples did not understand any of this. He writes, "Its meaning was hidden from them, and they did not know what he was talking about" (Luke 18:34).

Perhaps this is the reason why they continued to believe that Jesus would be a political messiah who would soon establish His rule on the earth. It is clear from what happened next that some of the disciples thought Jesus' rule was imminent. Certainly James and John and their mother thought that their opportunity for rulership was close at hand. The disciples' mother asked a favor of Jesus: "Grant that one of these two sons of mine may sit at your right and the other at your left in your kingdom" (Matthew 20:20–21).

Jesus replied that they did not know what they were asking. Knowing that rather than being made a king He was about to be killed, He told them that He could not assign positions of rulership that had been prepared by His Father.

When the other disciples heard what James and John and their mother had asked, they were upset. But Jesus called them all together and taught them a very important lesson about position and authority.

He said, "You know that the rulers of the Gentiles lord it over them, and their high officials exercise authority over them. Not so with you. Instead, whoever wants to become great among you must be your servant, and whoever wants to be first must be your slave—just as the Son of Man did not come to be served, but to serve, and to give his life as a ransom for many" (verses 24–28).

The Present and Future Messiah

Continuing on His way to Jerusalem from the Jordan Valley, Jesus had to pass by the ancient city of Jericho. The Gospels record three important events that took place while He was in the vicinity of the city.

First He healed two blind men. One of them was named Bartimaeus (Mark 10:46). When he heard the crowd going by, he asked what was happening and was told that Jesus of Nazareth was passing by. His response was to call out, "Jesus, Son of David, have mercy on me!" The fact that he would call Jesus "Son of David" is interesting in itself. It shows that he understood that Jesus was the Messiah. The title "Son of David" is a messianic title.

Jesus asked him, "What do you want me to do for you?"

"I want to see," he said.

Jesus said to him, "Receive your sight; your faith has healed you." At once both he and his companion were able to see, and they followed Jesus (Luke 18:35–43; Matthew 20:29–34).

Also at Jericho was a chief tax collector named Zacchaeus. He wanted to see who Jesus was, but because the crowd was so great and he was a short man, he climbed into a tree to obtain a clear view. As Jesus reached the place, he looked up and said immediately, "Zacchaeus, come down. . . . I must stay at your house today" (Luke 19:1–5).

The self-righteous in the crowd muttered, "He has gone to be the guest of a 'sinner.'" The response from Zacchaeus, though, was, "Look, Lord! Here and now I give half of my possessions to the poor, and if I have cheated anybody out of anything, I will pay back four times the amount." Zacchaeus's reaction was no doubt an embarrassment to the self-righteous. As Jesus said, "This man, too, is a son of Abraham. For the Son of Man came to seek and to save what was lost" (verses 6–10).

While He had their attention, He went on to explain that the kingdom of God was not going to appear immediately. Though He was on His way to Jerusalem, it did not mean that He was about to establish the kingdom of God.

He told them a parable about a man of noble birth who went to a distant country to have himself appointed king and then to return. Knowing that he would be gone for some time, he called 10 of his servants and gave them some money to invest.

The nobleman's subjects hated him and sent a delegation after him to say, "We don't want this man to be our king." But he was made king and returned. He sent for his servants to find out what they had done with the money he'd given them (verses 12–15).

The first two had invested, and the money had multiplied. But one of the servants had simply hidden the money, saying to himself that the master was a hard man and that he was afraid of him. The nobleman replied, "If you thought that I was a hard man, why didn't you put the money in the bank so that it could gain interest?" (verses 22–23, paraphrased).

The money was taken away and given to the servant who had produced most: "to everyone who has, more will be given, but as for the one who has nothing, even what he has will be taken away" (verse 26). The nobleman then commanded that those who did not want him to be king were to be killed in front of him.

Jesus told this story to show that His return was not imminent and that much was required of His followers in the meantime.

He then continued on His journey up to Jerusalem for the last Passover.

Chapter Nine

Inclusion and Exclusion

"The wedding banquet is ready, but those I invited did not deserve to come. Go to the street corners and invite to the banquet anyone you find." The servants went and brought anyone they could find, both good and bad, and filled the banquet hall.

Each year at the Passover season, large numbers of people went up from the country to Jerusalem.

By now Jesus had attracted so much attention with His teachings and miracles that people were looking for Him, especially in the temple area. The chief priests and the Pharisees had already plotted to kill Him and had given orders that anyone seeing Him should report it so that He could be arrested. When Jesus was not to be found at the temple, the people began to speculate that He might not come to the feast that year.

In fact, Jesus had arrived at Bethany, just outside Jerusalem, six days before the Passover. It was there that He had raised His friend Lazarus from the dead. Now a large crowd came to see not only Jesus but also the resurrected man.

The focus of attention on Lazarus caused the chief priests to make plans to kill him as well, because, as John's Gospel says, "on account of him many of the Jews were going over to Jesus and putting their faith in him" (John 12:11).

The next day Jesus sent two of His disciples to find a donkey and her colt and to bring them to Him. He then rode toward Jerusalem on the colt. The crowds took palm fronds and met Him, shouting, "Blessed is he who comes in the name of the Lord!" "Blessed is the King of Israel!" (verse 13). All of this was a fulfillment of an ancient prophecy recorded in Isaiah and also in Zechariah: "Say to the Daughter of Zion, 'See, your king comes to you, gentle and riding on a donkey, on a colt, the foal of a donkey'" (Matthew 21:4–5; see also Isaiah 62:11 and Zechariah 9:9).

The word was now quickly spreading that Jesus, the man who had raised Lazarus from the dead, was entering Jerusalem in fulfillment of a messianic prophecy. The

Pharisees were frustrated. "This is getting us nowhere," they said. "Look how the whole world has gone after him!" (John 12:19). They told Jesus to rebuke His disciples for acclaiming Him the Messiah. Jesus said simply, "If they keep quiet, the stones will cry out" (Luke 19:40).

As He approached Jerusalem from the Mount of Olives, Jesus saw the city ahead of Him and began to weep, knowing the destruction that it would face from the Romans in a few years. He said, "If you, even you, had only known on this day what would bring you peace—but now it is hidden from your eyes. The days will come upon you when your enemies will build an embankment against you and encircle you and hem you in on every side. They will dash you to the ground, you and the children within your walls. They will not leave one stone on another, because you did not recognize the time of God's coming to you" (verses 42–44).

By the time Jesus entered Jerusalem and went to the temple, the whole city was excited. The blind and the lame came for healing. The children were shouting, "Hosanna to the Son of David" (Matthew 21:14–15).

The chief priests and scribes were indignant. "Do you hear what these children are saying?" they protested.

"Yes," Jesus replied. He then asked them, quoting from Psalm 8, "Have you never read, 'From the lips of children and infants you have ordained praise'?" (Matthew 21:16).

Time Grows Short

Following His dramatic entry into the city, Jesus returned to Bethany. On His way back to Jerusalem the next day He was hungry, and seeing a fig tree in leaf, He went to find out whether it had any fruit on it. Jesus knew that the

Passover season was not the time for figs, but He used the circumstance to teach a lesson.

In the Hebrew Scriptures the fig tree is sometimes used to symbolize Israel. Jesus' own people had produced little fruit of the spiritual kind. Now He cursed the tree (verse 19), saying, "May you never bear fruit again!"—symbolic of the coming destruction of Jerusalem.

When He arrived at the temple, Jesus for the second time drove out the merchants who were buying and selling. He overturned the moneychangers' tables and the benches of those selling sacrificial doves. He prevented anyone carrying merchandise through the courts of the temple. Instead of the temple being a house of prayer for all nations, it had become a den of robbers—a gathering place for merchants who, for the sake of personal financial gain, took unfair advantage of those coming there to worship and to offer sacrifices.

For several days Jesus continued to teach at the temple. The chief priests and scribes and the leaders of the people became more and more hateful, yet they could not find a way to kill Him.

Some of the Greek-speaking worshipers who had come from outside Judea for the Passover asked the disciple Philip if they could see Jesus. Their request seemed to remind Jesus of His earlier words to the Jews, when He told them that He would be with them only a short time (John 7:33–34). He simply said, "The hour has come for the Son of Man to be glorified" (John 12:23).

Jesus acknowledged that He was deeply troubled by His impending death but knew that He could not ask His Father to save Him at that time, because as He said, "for this very reason I came to this hour" (verse 27).

Suddenly the crowd heard a loud noise. Some said it was thunder, while others said an angel had spoken to Him. Jesus said, "This voice was for your benefit, not mine" (verse 30). He then showed them what kind of death He was going to have to die. He spoke of being "lifted up."

The crowds asked, "We have heard from the Law that the Christ will remain forever, so how can you say, 'The Son of Man must be lifted up'? Who is this 'Son of Man'?"

Jesus replied that they should pay attention to Him as long as they had Him with them. He said, "Put your trust in the light while you have it, so that you may become sons of light" (verse 36). He then left and was nowhere to be found for a while.

Blinded by the Light

There were many who had seen Jesus' miraculous signs yet did not believe in Him. As John says, they fulfilled the prophecy in Isaiah: "He has blinded their eyes and deadened their hearts, so they can neither see with their eyes, nor understand with their hearts, nor turn—and I would heal them" (verse 40, based on Isaiah 6:10). Isaiah had understood what Jesus would do and had written about Him.

But the prophecy of spiritual blindness did not apply to everyone. Some of the Pharisees and leaders believed in Jesus but were too afraid of being put out of the synagogue to admit it.

These were the kinds of actions that caused Jesus to cry out, "When a man believes in me, he does not believe in me only, but in the one who sent me. When he looks at me, he sees the one who sent me. I have come into the world as a light, so that no one who believes in me should stay in darkness.

"As for the person who hears my words but does not keep them, I do not judge him. For I did not come to judge the world, but to save it. There is a judge for the one who rejects me and does not accept my words; that very word which I spoke will condemn him at the last day. For I did not speak of my own accord, but the Father who sent me commanded me what to say and how to say it. I know that his command leads to eternal life. So whatever I say is just what the Father has told me to say" (verses 44–50).

The next day, as they passed by the fig tree that Jesus had cursed earlier, Peter said, "Rabbi, look! The fig tree you cursed has withered!" (Mark 11:21).

Jesus replied, "I tell you the truth, if you have faith and do not doubt, not only can you do what was done to the fig tree, but also you can say to this mountain, 'Go, throw yourself into the sea,' and it will be done. If you believe, you will receive whatever you ask for in prayer" (Matthew 21:21–22).

Dishonest Leaders

The confrontation between Jesus and the chief priests, the teachers and the elders was coming to a conclusion. As He was teaching the people in the temple courts, the leaders came to Him and asked, "By what authority are you doing these things? And who gave you authority to do this?" (Mark 11:28). They were referring, no doubt, to His cleansing of the temple and to the continuing miracles He performed.

Jesus replied, "I will ask you one question. Answer me, and I will tell you by what authority I am doing these things." He asked them about John the Baptist, saying, "Was [his baptism] from heaven, or from men? Tell me!"

They discussed it among themselves and concluded that they could not say whether it was from God or from men. If they said it was from heaven, then they knew Christ would ask: Then why didn't you believe John? If they said it was from men, then the people would stone them, because the people recognized John as a prophet. So they had to avoid giving a truthful answer and said, "We don't know." Jesus responded, "Neither will I tell you by what authority I am doing these things" (verses 29–33).

He went on to give three parables to demonstrate the leaders' failure to recognize where God was working.

First He told a story about a man who had two sons. He asked the first to go and work in his vineyard. "I will not," he answered, but he later changed his mind and went. The father went to the other son and made the same request. He answered, "I will, sir," but he did not go. "Which of the two did what his father wanted?" Jesus asked. "The first," they said. In so doing they condemned themselves, because they were like the second son: they said they believed in God, but they didn't do what He asked of them (Matthew 21:28–31a).

Referring again to John the Baptist, Jesus said, "I tell you the truth, the tax collectors and the prostitutes are entering the kingdom of God ahead of you. For John came to you to show you the way of righteousness, and you did not believe him, but the tax collectors and the prostitutes did. And even after you saw this, you did not repent and believe him" (verses 31b–32).

Next Jesus told a parable about a landowner who planted a vineyard and rented it out to some farmers while he went on a journey. At harvest time the landowner sent his servants to collect some of the fruit of the vineyard. The tenant farmers beat one servant, killed another and stoned the third. The landowner sent other servants, more than the first time, but the tenant farmers again beat some and killed others. With only one person left to send, the landowner told himself, "They will respect my son," and sent him.

When they saw him, however, the tenant farmers talked the matter over and said, "This is the heir. Come, let's kill him, and the inheritance will be ours" (Mark 12:1–7). So they killed him and threw him out of the vineyard. Now Jesus asked His audience, "When the landowner comes, what do you think he will do to the tenants? He will kill them and give the vineyard to others" (verse 9, paraphrased).

The people were shocked by the story and said, "May this never be!" (Luke 20:16b).

Jesus looked at them directly, saying, "Then what is the meaning of that which is written: 'The stone the builders rejected has become the capstone'?" (verse 17). He concluded by telling the leaders that the kingdom of God would be taken away from them and given to a people who would produce its fruit.

Speaking of Himself, He said, "He who falls on this stone [the capstone] will be broken to pieces, but he on whom it falls will be crushed" (Matthew 21:44).

Now the chief priests and teachers of the law, knowing that Jesus had spoken the two parables against them, tried to find a way to arrest Him immediately. But they decided against it, because they were afraid of the people.

Jesus now spoke a third parable about the kingdom of heaven: A king prepared a wedding banquet for his son. He sent servants to those who had been invited, telling them to come, but they refused. So he sent more servants with the news that the meal was ready. Still the invited guests paid no attention. Some simply went about their own business, while others attacked the king's servants and killed them.

Naturally the king was angry, so he sent his army to destroy his enemies and burn their city. He said to his servants, "The wedding banquet is ready, but those I invited did not deserve to come. Go to the street corners and invite to the banquet anyone you find." The servants went and brought anyone they could find, both good and bad, and filled the banquet hall (Matthew 22:1–10).

When the king came in he noticed that one man was not wearing wedding clothes. "Friend," he asked, "how did you get in here without wedding clothes?" The man had nothing to say. Then the king told his servants, "Tie him hand and foot, and throw him outside, into the darkness, where there will be weeping and gnashing of teeth. For many are invited, but few are chosen" (verses 11–14).

Clearly Jesus was doubly emphasizing the rejection of the religious leadership of His time because they had rejected Him.

A Change of Rulership

The more time went by in the week before Jesus' final Passover, the more the religious leadership tried to corner Him. Perhaps He could be trapped into saying something illegal.

Two groups—the Pharisees and the Herodians—who would not normally have been in alliance, came to Him and said, "Teacher, we know you are a man of integrity and that you teach the way of God in accordance with the truth. You aren't swayed by men, because you pay no attention to who they are. Tell us then, what is your opinion? Is it right to pay taxes to Caesar or not?" (verses 16–17).

But Jesus saw through their duplicity and replied, "You hypocrites, why are you trying to trap me? Show me the coin used for paying the tax." The coin had Caesar's head imprinted on it. So Jesus continued, "Give to Caesar what is Caesar's, and to God what is God's" (verses 18–21). With this He silenced them.

The same day another religious group, the Sadducees, tested Him with a question about the resurrection. They invited Him to give His opinion as to what would happen to a woman who married seven brothers in succession. After all, according to the law of Moses it was a theoretical possibility when a man died without an heir. They asked, "At the resurrection whose wife will she be, since the seven were married to her?" (Luke 20:27–33).

It was interesting that the Sadducees should ask about the resurrection, because they didn't believe in it. Jesus showed them that they didn't know the Scriptures or the power of God and were therefore mistaken in their understanding. He taught them that at the resurrection, people will neither marry nor be given in marriage. Correcting their erroneous view, Jesus quoted the book of Exodus, where God spoke to Moses, saying, "I am the God of Abraham, the God of Isaac, and the God of Jacob." Jesus added, "He is not the God of the dead, but of the living. You are badly mistaken!" (Mark 12:24–27). Once again people were left speechless by His explanations.

Then a Pharisee asked, "Teacher, which is the greatest commandment in the Law?" Jesus replied that there are two great commands that encapsulate the law. The first is to "love the Lord your God with all your heart and with all your soul and with all your mind." He said, "This is the first and greatest commandment. And the second is like it: 'Love your neighbor as yourself.'" Then He added, "All the Law and the Prophets hang on these two commandments" (Matthew 22:35–40).

The Pharisee was impressed. Jesus noted that the man had understood well and told him, "You are not far from the kingdom of God" (Mark 12:34).

After this no one dared ask Him any more questions.

Jesus then directed the discussion to the relationship between Christ and David. Observing that in the book of Psalms David calls Christ "Lord," Jesus asked how Christ could then be the son of David (Luke 20:41–44).

This was the kind of puzzling question that delighted the crowd and silenced the religious leaders. It was an opportunity for Jesus to explain to the people that, while the scribes and Pharisees had ecclesiastical authority, they were not to be followed in their hypocrisy.

He said: "They tie up heavy loads and put them on men's shoulders, but they themselves are not willing to lift a finger to move them. Everything they do is done for men to see" (Matthew 23:1–5a).

He commented on their flowing robes and on their desire for recognition in the street and for the most important seats in the synagogue and at banquets. He added that they were overly concerned with money and appearance, saying, "Such men will be punished most severely" (verses 5b–7; Luke 20:46–47).

Jesus taught that men are not to be given titles like "Rabbi," because only Christ is the Master. Neither are we to call anyone on earth "Father," since we have only one Father, in heaven. Nor are we to be reverentially called "Teacher," for we have only one Teacher, Jesus Christ, who stressed humility among leaders (Matthew 23:8–12).

Next Jesus expressed His disgust for the scribes and Pharisees with seven statements that begin with the word *woe*. He characterized them as hypocrites, blind guides, blind fools, blind Pharisees, whitewashed tombs, snakes and vipers. This is the most powerful indictment of the religious hierarchy recorded in His entire ministry.

Of Jerusalem itself, Jesus said that the inhabitants had killed the prophets and stoned to death those God had sent. He said that He had longed to gather Jerusalem's children together, but they had been unwilling. Now the city would be left desolate and they would not see Him again until they could say, "Blessed is he who comes in the name of the Lord" (verse 39), a reference to His second coming.

As Jesus sat and watched the rich putting their gifts into the temple treasury, He also noticed a poor widow putting in two very small copper coins worth less than a penny. He said to His disciples, "I tell you the truth, this poor widow has put more into the treasury than all the others. They all gave out of their wealth; but she, out of her poverty, put in everything—all she had to live on" (Mark 12:41–44). It was another condemnation of the wealthy, corrupt and hypocritical religious leadership, who in fact were burdening the poor into giving more than they could afford.

The End of the World?

As they were leaving the temple enclosure, Jesus' disciples drew His attention to the magnificence of Herodian

Jerusalem. It was a city built in the Roman style as a tribute by the house of Herod to their imperial overlords.

One of the disciples said, "Look, Teacher! What massive stones! What magnificent buildings!"

But Jesus was evidently not impressed with the apparent permanence of the buildings. Knowing what was in Jerusalem's near future, He said, "Do you see all these great buildings? Not one stone here will be left on another; every one will be thrown down" (Mark 13:1–2).

Arriving at the Mount of Olives, Peter, James, John and Andrew asked Him in private, "Tell us, when will these things be? And what will be the sign of Your coming, and of the end of the age?" (Matthew 24:3, NKJV). They knew that Christ would return as King of kings and Lord of lords. But the question was, when would that happen? They could not help but think that Jesus' prediction of the destruction of Jerusalem's magnificent temple and its surroundings would come only when the world as they knew it would end.

Jesus said: "Take heed that no one deceives you. For many will come in My name, saying, 'I am the Christ,' and will deceive many." Jesus first gave a warning that many would come claiming His position as Messiah and the returning Lord of lords, and would deceive many (verses 4–5, NKJV).

Now, most people are not deceived by the religiously deluded who think they are Christ. When we see such people or hear their claims, we conclude that they are deceived. So what did Christ mean when He said we should beware those who say "I am the Christ"?

In the past century Stalin, Mussolini, Hitler, Mao Zedong and other political leaders believed they could solve their nation's woes. Each believed that he was the anointed one to solve all of his people's problems. In a counterfeit of what Jesus Christ will do at His return, Adolf Hitler began what he said would be a 1,000-year Reich, or kingdom. Mussolini declared himself the great Lawgiver, the Super Hero. These men and others like them through the centuries have deceived many with their preposterous, inflated claims to omnipotence.

It is as Christ said it would be. What they have done in their folly is attempt to usurp Christ's own future role of ruling the world in peace and harmony. There is only one Messiah. He has come once, and He is yet to come again to set up the kingdom of God on this earth.

Signs of the Times

Jesus continued His reply to the disciples' question about the timing and evidence of His return and the end of the age by warning them not to fear every war and revolution that happens. He said that such things would have to occur in the course of events. They do not necessarily mean that the end of the age is imminent. In fact, He said, "such things must happen, but the end is still to come" (verse 6). "Nation will rise against nation, and kingdom against kingdom. There will be great earthquakes, famines and pestilences in various places, and fearful events and great signs from heaven" (Luke 21:10–11).

There would also be persecution of believers. He said to His followers, "You must be on your guard. You will be handed over to the local councils and flogged in the synagogues. On account of me you will stand before governors and kings as witnesses to them" (Mark 13:9).

They were not to worry about what to say under such circumstances. The Holy Spirit would help them at the time. But the end of the age would still not have arrived.

The next thing Jesus listed was that even family members would betray each other in the progression toward the end of the age of human rule. Further He said, "All men will hate you because of me. But not a hair of your head will perish. By standing firm you will gain life" (Luke 21:16–19).

He also warned that there would be an increase of false prophets, deceiving many people with their predictions and teachings. Then people's natural affection for each other would begin to fail in an onrush of immorality and wickedness. But the good news of God's coming kingdom would be announced in all the world as the only hope for a solution to humanity's problems. Then, Jesus said, the end of human misrule would come.

The disciples had asked Jesus a question that has resonated ever since. It is, in a sense, one of the ultimate questions: When will this age of man end? People have asked the question in other ways, such as "Is the world about to end?" and "Is there a crisis so overwhelming that it will end the world?" In this day of man-made catastrophes and predictions of ecological doom, it is not an unfamiliar thought.

The Desolation of Jerusalem

Next, Jesus gave some details about events in the Middle East before His return. These are not generalities. According to the Gospel writer Mark, Jesus said, "'So when you see the "abomination of desolation," spoken of by Daniel the prophet, standing where it ought not' (let the reader understand), 'then let those who are in Judea flee to the mountains'" (Mark 13:14, NKJV).

Matthew's Gospel records almost the same words, while Luke refers only to armies surrounding Jerusalem and mentions that the desolation of the city is near. The same Greek word for "desolation" is used for both the abomination and the armies. This leads to the thought that it is the armies surrounding Jerusalem that are the desecration. Another explanation is that either an idol or a person is set in a holy place in Jerusalem, making the location desolate by its presence.

Yet we are also to be aware that the book of the prophet Daniel has something to tell us about these matters. The book provides much prophetic information about the pollution of the temple at Jerusalem in 167 B.C.E. by the unpredictable king of Syria, Antiochus Epiphanes. So in the minds of His biographers, Jesus was making a connection between Daniel's account of Jerusalem's history and what will yet occur there.

Antiochus had set up an altar to Zeus over the altar of burnt offering at the temple. He had gone as far as to sacrifice a pig on that altar. (The pig is, of course, one of the unclean animals listed in the Law.) In this way he desecrated the precincts of the temple. This was the original abomination of desolation.

Something similar would happen again, since Antiochus was a prophetic type of a future antichrist. In 70 C.E. the Roman armies destroyed the temple and much of Herodian Jerusalem. In 135 the emperor Hadrian began the rebuilding of Jerusalem as a Hellenistic, gentile city, naming it Aelia Capitolina. He installed a statue of himself on the Temple Mount.

There is yet a third fulfillment of the abomination of desolation to come, because the final antichrist figure will be alive at the time of the Second Coming.

A Question of Survival

When Jesus spoke of these matters, He was giving specifics based on previously fulfilled prophecy that will also have a future fulfillment. When these things begin to happen, Jesus said that those in Jerusalem should flee for their lives to the mountains. Those mountains are across the Jordan River. History records that early followers of Jesus did flee to Pella, now in northern Jordan, just before the 70 C.E. destruction of Jerusalem. The city was surrounded by armies—Roman legions—and it was certainly left desolate.

There will be a future time when the inhabitants should once again leave the city for their own survival. Looking to the final fulfillment, Jesus said, "How dreadful it will be in those days for pregnant women and nursing mothers! Pray that your flight will not take place in winter or on the Sabbath." He went on to say that there will be no worse time in human history, "for then there will be great distress, unequaled from the beginning of the world until now—and never to be equaled again. If those days had not been cut short, no one would survive, but for the sake of the elect those days will be shortened" (Matthew 24:19–22).

Thankfully those days will be cut short by God's own intervention, because God will act to preserve human life from extinction.

At that time there will be false prophets who will say that Christ has already returned. But they will be wrong, because His return will be very evident to all, not a secret. As He said, "For as lightning that comes from the east is visible even in the west, so will be the coming of the Son of Man" (verse 27). People want to know, what is the sign of His coming? Here is Christ's own answer. It will be like lightning flashing across the sky. It will be preceded by startling occurrences in the heavens and on earth. Notice this description: "There will be signs in the sun, moon and stars. On the earth, nations will be in anguish and perplexity at the roaring and tossing of the sea" (Luke 21:25).

Then finally humanity will see the sign that so many have looked for. Jesus said, "At that time the sign of the Son of Man will appear in the sky, and all the nations of the earth will mourn. They will see the Son of Man coming on the clouds of the sky, with power and great glory. And he will send his angels with a loud trumpet call, and they will gather his elect from the four winds, from one end of the heavens to the other" (Matthew 24:30–31).

This, then, was Jesus' specific lengthy response to when the end would come and how He would return.

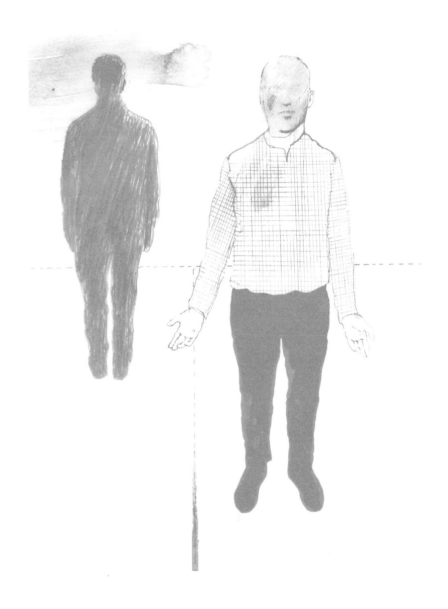

Chapter Ten

Belief and Positive Action

Eternal life and eternal punishment will ultimately be decided on the basis of our attitude to God and our fellow human beings, as proven by our actions. Will we keep the two great commands of the law that Jesus spoke of when He addressed the rich young man who wanted eternal life?

Toward the end of His ministry, Jesus gave a harrowing description of what world conditions would be like prior to His second coming. He went on to explain what His followers should do in preparation for that time, whenever it would come.

He said we should learn a lesson from the fig tree. Just as we can tell that summer is near when the leaves come out, we can know in general terms when Jesus' return will happen by the fact that all of the conditions He described have been met.

He noted that a single generation would see the fulfillment of all the prophesied events. It makes sense, then, that the various wars, earthquakes, famines and persecutions that have happened over the past 2,000 years have not signaled the ultimate end; they have been precursors. Furthermore, the disturbances that are prophesied to occur in the heavens have not yet taken place.

The return of Jesus Christ is not a myth; it is a reality that has not yet occurred. However, as Jesus pointed out, it is impossible to predict the exact timing of His return. He said that even He is not party to when it will be ("No one knows about that day or hour, not even the angels in heaven, nor the Son, but only the Father" [Matthew 24:36]).

However, He did give some indications of the way the world would be in attitude and approach at that time. He said, "As it was in the days of Noah, so it will be at the coming of the Son of Man. For in the days before the flood, people were eating and drinking, marrying and giving in marriage, up to the day Noah entered the ark; and they knew nothing about what would happen until the flood came and took them all away. That is how it will be at the coming of the Son of Man" (verses 37–39). In other words, most people will continue doing the things they normally do, seemingly oblivious of what will be just ahead, despite the warnings they will hear. The few who heed the warnings will escape.

Lessons in Vigilance

Jesus also gave five parables to help us understand the importance of faithfulness and being personally vigilant. He said that we should be on guard—keep watch—because we do not know on what day He will return. He said, "It's like a man going away: He leaves his house and puts his servants in charge, each with his assigned task, and tells the one at the door to keep watch" (Mark 13:34).

As we anticipate His return, we are to "be careful, or [our] hearts will be weighed down with dissipation, drunkenness and the anxieties of life, and that day will close on [us] unexpectedly like a trap. For it will come upon all those who live on the face of the whole earth" (Luke 21:34–35). Here, then, is information for all: "What I say to you, I say to everyone: 'Watch!'" (Mark 13:37).

The second parable concerned watching for a thief. Jesus said, "If the owner of the house had known at what time of night the thief was coming, he would have kept watch and would not have let his house be broken into. So you also must be ready, because the Son of Man will come at an hour when you do not expect him" (Matthew 24:43–44).

In a third, lengthier example, Jesus spoke of a servant who had been put in charge of the other servants' needs while his master was away. He said, "Who then is the faithful and wise servant, whom the master has put in charge of the servants in his household to give them their food at the proper time? It will be good for that servant whose master finds him doing so when he returns" (verses 45–46). The emphasis here is on faithful service until Jesus' return.

But there is also a warning for those tempted to say that the Second Coming is in the far future. Jesus continued, "But suppose that servant is wicked and says to himself, 'My master is staying away a long time,' and he then begins to beat his fellow servants and to eat and drink with drunkards. The master of that servant will come on a day when he does not expect him and at an hour he is not aware of. He will cut him to pieces and assign him a place with the hypocrites, where there will be weeping and gnashing of teeth" (verses 48–51).

The fourth parable to emphasize watchfulness is the famous parable of the ten virgins, five of whom were wise and five foolish. They were waiting for a bridegroom to come. Half of them took no extra oil for their lamps. The other half had a supply with them. There was a delay in the bridegroom's arrival, and they all fell asleep. At midnight an announcement was made that he had arrived. Only half of them were prepared with oil in their lamps to go out and meet him. The others desperately tried to buy oil, but it was too late. The bridegroom arrived while they were unprepared. They tried later to get in to the wedding banquet but were kept out: the bridegroom said, "I don't know you" (Matthew 25:1–13). Again it was a warning to be vigilant, because the precise timing of Jesus' return is not known.

The fifth and final parable about faithfulness concerned a man going on a journey and giving money to his servants to use until his return. Jesus said, "To one he gave five talents of money, to another two talents, and to another one talent, each according to his ability. Then he went on his journey. The man who had received the five talents went at once and put his money to work and gained five more. So also, the one with the two talents gained two more. But the man who had received the one talent went off, dug a hole in the ground and hid his master's money" (verses 14–18).

When the master returned, those who had increased their holdings were rewarded with more. They had been faithful. But the one who had operated out of fear of his master and had done nothing, had his money taken away and given to the one who had the 10 talents. The faithless servant was said to be worthless in the parable.

As we anticipate the return of Jesus Christ, then, it is clear that vigilance and faithfulness are prerequisites.

Life and Death Forever

Jesus had answered at length His disciples' questions about the end of the age and His return to rule as King of kings. Now in conclusion He spoke of the judgment that will occur after His second coming. It was an unexpected end to His conversation, yet it connected His followers with their personal responsibility as they waited for their Master's return.

Jesus said, "When the Son of Man comes in his glory, and all the angels with him, he will sit on his throne. . . . All the nations will be gathered before him, and he will separate the people one from another as a shepherd separates the sheep from the goats. He will put the sheep on his right and the goats on his left" (Matthew 25:31–33). This ruler will have authority over the nations, and He will judge them according to an interesting standard, as Jesus pointed out next.

He said, "Then the King will say to those on his right, 'Come, you who are blessed by my Father; take your inheritance, the kingdom prepared for you since the creation of the world. For I was hungry and you gave me something to eat, I was thirsty and you gave me something to drink, I was a stranger and you invited me in, I needed clothes and you clothed me, I was sick and you looked after me, I was in prison and you came to visit me'" (verses 34–36). As Jesus said, His followers had done this to fellow man, and by so doing, it was as if they had performed that service to Jesus Himself.

To those who have not done such service to others, the King of kings will say, "Depart from me, you who are cursed, into the eternal fire prepared for the devil and his angels. For I was hungry and you gave me nothing to eat, I was thirsty and you gave me nothing to drink, I was a stranger and you did not invite me in, I needed clothes and you did not clothe me, I was sick and in prison and you did not look after me" (verses 41–43).

Eternal life and eternal punishment will ultimately be decided on the basis of our attitude to God and our fellow human beings, as proven by our actions. Will we keep the two great commands of the law that Jesus spoke of when He addressed the rich young man who wanted eternal life? Will we love God and our fellow man?

Of Greed and Betrayal

When Jesus had finished this lengthy discussion with His disciples, He reminded them that the Passover was two days away and that His death was imminent.

The religious authorities were looking for a way to capture and murder Him. Matthew's Gospel says, "Then the chief priests and the elders of the people assembled in the palace of the high priest, whose name was Caiaphas, and they plotted to arrest Jesus in some sly way and kill him. 'But not during the Feast,' they said, 'or there may be a riot among the people'" (Matthew 26:3–5).

Jesus was staying close to Jerusalem, at Bethany, with His friends Mary and Martha and their brother, Lazarus. One evening they were together at the home of a man named Simon, when Mary took some expensive perfume and poured it on Jesus. Some in the group were upset at what they perceived to be a waste. They said it could have been sold and the money given to the poor.

One of the complainers was Judas Iscariot, the man who was soon to betray Jesus to the authorities. But as John's Gospel shows, Judas's motives were far from pure. John says, "He did not say this because he cared about the poor but because he was a thief; as keeper of the money bag, he used to help himself to what was put into it" (John 12:6).

Jesus' responded to this accusation of waste on Mary's part: "Leave her alone. Why are you bothering her? She has done a beautiful thing to me. The poor you will always have with you, and you can help them any time you want. But you will not always have me. She did what she could. She poured perfume on my body beforehand to prepare for my burial. I tell you the truth, wherever the gospel is preached throughout the world, what she has done will also be told, in memory of her" (Mark 14:6–9).

Judas, however, was not satisfied. The next we read of him is when he has decided to betray Jesus to the authorities. Going to them, he asked what they would pay for such a betrayal. They gave him 30 pieces of silver. Judas now set about finding the right opportunity to deliver Jesus when there was no crowd present. Despite the authorities' earlier commitment not to take Jesus at the Passover because of the crowds and Jesus' popularity, Judas's offer was too good to refuse.

Who Is the Greatest?

The last Passover that Jesus kept with His disciples was held in an upper room in Jerusalem. On a Tuesday evening Jesus and the disciples came together to observe the most solemn of the biblical observances.

When they were seated, Jesus said, "I have eagerly desired to eat this Passover with you before I suffer. For I tell you, I will not eat it again until it finds fulfillment in the kingdom of God" (Luke 22:15–16). It was a signal that His death was imminent. His disciples still did not seem to understand the significance of what He was saying, as is illustrated by what happened next.

An argument broke out among them as to who was the greatest. Jesus explained, as He had before, that it was service that marked out the righteous leaders among them, not lordship and authority of the world's kind. He said, "But you are not to be like that. Instead, the greatest among you should be like the youngest, and the one who rules like the one who serves. For who is greater, the one who is at the table or the one who serves? Is it not the one who is at the table? But I am among you as one who serves" (verses 26–27).

Directing their sights toward the great goal ahead, He reminded them that they would be in His kingdom with Him. He said, "You are those who have stood by me in my trials. And I confer on you a kingdom, just as my Father conferred one on me, so that you may eat and drink at my table in my kingdom and sit on thrones, judging the twelve tribes of Israel" (verses 28–30).

An Act of Greatness

To emphasize the humility that would be necessary for them to deal with each other and with their fellow human beings, Jesus got up from the table, took off His outer clothing, wrapped a towel around His waist, and began to wash their feet.

This was a menial task typically performed only by household servants. Yet here was their Master doing exactly that. They had been debating their greatness; now He was showing them by a physical example how they should be in spirit. This was far from the self-exaltation they had just indulged in.

He came to Peter, who asked in a somewhat perplexed tone, "Lord, are you going to wash my feet?" (John 13:6). As Jesus said, Peter did not yet understand the significance, but he would. Once Jesus told him that he must not refuse or he would have no part with Him, Peter replied that he now wanted to be washed completely. Jesus pointed out that washing his feet would be sufficient.

When He had finished the task, Jesus asked them whether they understood what He had just done. He said, "You call me 'Teacher' and 'Lord,' and rightly so, for that is what I am. Now that I, your Lord and Teacher, have washed your feet, you also should wash one another's feet. I have set you an example that you should do as I have done for you. I tell you the truth, no servant is greater than his master, nor is a messenger greater than the one who sent him. Now that you know these things, you will be blessed if you do them" (verses 13–17).

Here, then, Jesus set a new tradition for the Church that they would observe after His return to the Father. One of the practices they would follow would be to wash each other's feet in an annual ceremony commemorating Jesus' life of service and sacrifice for humanity.

True Discipleship

Jesus knew, however, that at the table was someone who was not truly committed. He said, "One of you is going to betray me" (verse 21). This upset the disciples, and they began to question themselves. Peter signaled to John that he should ask Jesus who it was. Jesus said, "It is the one to whom I will give this piece of bread when I have dipped it in the dish." He then gave it to Judas Iscariot, saying, "What you are about to do, do quickly" (verses 26–27). But the others thought that Judas had to buy something for the Passover season, since he was the treasurer.

Judas left, and Jesus, knowing what was about to happen, said, "Now is the Son of Man glorified and God is glorified in him. If God is glorified in him, God will glorify the Son in himself, and will glorify him at once" (verses 31–32).

Jesus then told them that He had only a little time left with them. He took the opportunity to give them a new commandment, that they should love each other. If they would do this, then all would know who they were—that they were His followers. But He said that first, that very night, they would all desert Him. Peter said he would never desert Jesus. But Jesus had to tell him the painful truth that before the cock would crow, Peter would have denied his Master three times.

Recasting the Passover

Once Judas was gone, Jesus instituted an amended Passover service that changed it from an Old Testament observance to a New Testament memorial. He emphasized the taking of bread and wine as an annual reminder of His own sacrifice for our sins. Mark tells us in his Gospel account: "And as they were eating, Jesus took bread, blessed and broke it, and gave it to them and said, 'Take, eat; this is My body.' Then He took the cup, and when He had given thanks He gave it to them, and they all drank from it. And He said to them, 'This is My blood of the new covenant, which is shed for many. Assuredly, I say to you, I will no longer drink of the fruit of the vine until that day when I drink it new in the kingdom of God'" (Mark 14:22–25, NKJV).

The annual commemoration of the New Testament Passover is an obligation for all true followers of Christ. As the apostle Paul later said, "For whenever you eat this bread and drink this cup, you proclaim the Lord's death until he comes" (1 Corinthians 11:26). When Jesus instituted the amended Passover on the evening before His death, He set the example for all who would truly follow Him.

Connected to the Vine

After conducting the Passover ceremony emphasizing the symbolism of bread and wine, Jesus took time to share with His disciples some final thoughts. As He had answered their questions on the Mount of Olives about the eventual end of the age, so He now told them what was going to happen immediately.

He said He was going away to prepare a place for them so they could be with Him in the future, and that they knew the way there. It was an enigmatic statement. Thomas gave voice to their puzzlement, saying, "We don't know where you are going, so how can we know the way?" Jesus replied, "I am the way and the truth and the life" (John 14:5–6). In other words, Jesus was making it clear that their new way of life would be one of following His example. The result of living that way would be to share in Christ's kingdom when it would be established on the earth.

Jesus went on to say that no one could come to understand God, the Father, except through Him. He said that by knowing Him, they could know the Father. This caused Philip to ask to see the Father. He said, "Show us the Father and that will be enough for us."

Jesus pointed out that they had experienced the Father by being with His Son for many months. What Jesus had said and done were the words and works of the Father. Jesus' miracles were evidence of the Father at work in the world. The relationship between the Father and the Son meant that the disciples could achieve greater works, because Christ would grant their requests for help from His position as the Son of God.

Jesus went on to explain that their love for Him would mean obedience to His commands. They had seen Him observe His Father's law, and they were required to do the same.

He then promised that the Father would send them spiritual comfort and help in the form of the Holy Spirit. The Holy Spirit is also the spirit of truth, unaccepted by the world at large. Soon Jesus would be gone, yet the disciples would not be like orphaned children, because the Holy Spirit would be with them.

Love and Obedience

After Jesus repeated the need to follow His commands as evidence of their love for Him and the Father, one of the disciples, named Judas (not the one who betrayed Him), asked why Jesus was not letting the world know who He was. Again His reply was enigmatic. He said that those who loved Him would obey His teaching and as a result would have a relationship with the Father also.

Jesus also said that He spoke only His Father's words, that the Holy Spirit would continue to reveal truth to them, and that they should be at peace and not be afraid. The disciples would go on in the world without His physical presence. Yet they would be making progress toward the eventual kingdom of God on the earth. They would contend with the pressures of living in this world for a time, comforted and helped by the Holy Spirit.

Jesus then warned them that Satan was about to attempt to thwart God's plan by having Him killed. Yet as He said, Satan, the prince of this world, would have no hold over Him. To demonstrate the Father's and the Son's unity of purpose, it was necessary that Jesus die willingly for the sins of humanity.

From now on the disciples' involvement with Jesus and all that He stood for would have to be total. He taught them that they were like branches of a vine. He was the vine and His Father was the gardener. Branches that bear no fruit are cut off. Branches that do bear fruit are pruned so that they can bear more fruit.

Productive disciples are like fruitful branches; they will need to be pruned at times so they can bear more fruit. The key to being fruitful is to stay connected to Christ, the vine. Jesus said, "Without Me you can do nothing" (John 15:5, NKJV).

He went on to explain again that obedience to His commands is essential: "If you obey my commands, you will remain in my love, just as I have obeyed my Father's commands and remain in his love" (verse 10). He then commanded the disciples to love one another as He, Christ, had loved them. He demonstrated the depth of that love by dying for them and for us. As He said, "Greater love has no one than this, that he lay down his life for his friends" (verse 13).

He reminded them that they had been drafted into service. Like all those God calls, they did not choose Him; He chose them to go out and bear fruit.

Practicing Faith

Jesus next explained that following Him meant separation from the world. Not the separation of the monastery or as a hermit, because Jesus intended that His followers would continue to live in society. His followers would be separated from the world by practicing His teachings.

He said, "If the world hates you, keep in mind that it hated me first. If you belonged to the world, it would love you as its own. As it is, you do not belong to the world, but I have chosen you out of the world. That is why the world hates you" (verses 18–19).

The hatred that the disciples would experience was the result of their enemies' not knowing God the Father, nor recognizing His Son. Jesus said the society around had seen His miracles and rejected both Him and His Father. He said this was the fulfillment of a prophecy in the book of Psalms, which says, "They hated me without reason" (verse 25).

Jesus went on to explain that the disciples would testify as witnesses of His work under the guidance of the Holy Spirit. He told them these things so they would not be discouraged by hostility and hatred. "They will put you out of the synagogue," He said; "in fact, a time is coming when anyone who kills you will think he is offering a service to God" (John 16:2).

So it is possible for people to think they are serving God when in fact they do not even know who He is.

Facing Opposition

Jesus again reassured His disciples that the Holy Spirit would come to help them, but only after He had left them. He would no longer be physically present with them, but the Holy Spirit would be given to them. The Spirit of God would guide them into all truth, inspiring them to understand the things of God.

Once again He reminded them that soon they would see Him no more, and then after a little while they would see Him. He spoke of going to the Father, but they couldn't understand what He meant. He explained further by saying, "You will weep and mourn while the world rejoices. You will grieve, but your grief will turn to joy. A woman giving birth to a child has pain because her time has come; but when her baby is born she forgets the anguish because of her joy that a child is born into the world" (verses 20–21).

Jesus was speaking of His soon-coming death and resurrection. He admitted that in all this He had been speaking in hard-to-grasp figurative language. For example, when He spoke of going to His Father, they had not understood. Now He said, "A time is coming when I will no longer use this kind of language but will tell you plainly about my Father" (verse 25).

He continued: "The Father himself loves you because you have loved me and have believed that I came from God. I came from the Father and entered the world; now I am leaving the world and going back to the Father" (verses 27–28).

Finally the disciples seemed to understand. They said, "Now you are speaking clearly and without figures of speech. Now we can see that you know all things and that you do not even need to have anyone ask you questions. This makes us believe that you came from God" (verses 29–30). Despite their assurance, Jesus replied that a time was coming when they would scatter and desert Him.

He said that He had told them these things so they could be forewarned and have peace. Although they would have opposition, hatred and hostility in the world, they could be encouraged because He had overcome the world and its animosity.

A Prayer for the Disciples

As the time came for Jesus' betrayal, the Gospel accounts describe in detail four prayers that Jesus offered up. One was for His disciples, and the other three were for the strength to go through the ordeal of crucifixion.

John's Gospel records the first prayer, in the upper room where He and the disciples were gathered for the Passover. Jesus looked toward heaven and prayed: "Father, the time has come. Glorify your Son, that your Son may glorify you. For you granted him authority over all people that he might give eternal life to all those you have given him. Now this is eternal life: that they may know you, the only true God, and

Jesus Christ, whom you have sent. I have brought you glory on earth by completing the work you gave me to do. And now, Father, glorify me in your presence with the glory I had with you before the world began" (John 17:1–5).

Jesus said that He had delivered God's Word—His truth—to the disciples whom the Father had called out of the world. He said, "I pray for them. I am not praying for the world, but for those you have given me, for they are yours" (verse 9).

Knowing that He would not remain in human society much longer, He prayed for protection for His disciples, saying, "Holy Father, protect them by the power of your name—the name you gave me—so that they may be one as we are one" (verse 11b). He said: "My prayer is not that you take them out of the world but that you protect them from the evil one. They are not of the world, even as I am not of it. Sanctify them by the truth; your word is truth" (verses 15–17).

Jesus went on to extend His prayer to all of His followers down through time, saying: "My prayer is not for them alone. I pray also for those who will believe in me through their message, that all of them may be one, Father, just as you are in me and I am in you. May they also be in us so that the world may believe that you have sent me" (verses 20–21).

Jesus concluded His prayer for the disciples by acknowledging the difference between those called and the world around. He said, "Righteous Father, though the world does not know you, I know you, and they know that you have sent me. I have made you known to them, and will continue to make you known in order that the love you have for me may be in them and that I myself may be in them" (verses 25–26).

Three Prayers for Strength

Next they sang a hymn together and went out across the Kidron Valley to an olive grove called Gethsemane, on the side of the Mount of Olives. Jesus said to His disciples, "Sit here while I go over there and pray." Then, taking Peter, James and John with Him, He began to be very distressed and troubled. "My soul is overwhelmed with sorrow to the point of death," He told them. "Stay here and keep watch with me" (Matthew 26:36–38).

Withdrawing a little farther from them, He fell to the ground and prayed, "My Father, if it is possible, may this cup be taken from me. Yet not as I will, but as you will" (verse 39). Luke's Gospel tells us that an angel from heaven appeared and strengthened Him. Now in great anguish He prayed even more fervently, so that His sweat was like drops of blood falling to the ground (Luke 22:43–44).

He got up from praying and went back to His disciples, who had fallen asleep, exhausted from sorrow. He said to Peter, "Could you men not keep watch with me for one hour? Get up and pray so that you will not fall into temptation. The spirit is willing, but the body is weak" (Matthew 26:40–41; Luke 22:45–46).

Now for the second time at Gethsemane He prayed, "My Father, if it is not possible for this cup to be taken away unless I drink it, may your will be done" (Matthew 26:42). Separation from the Father through death for sin was soon to be Christ's ultimate anguish.

When He went back to His disciples He found them asleep again. This time they didn't know what to say, so He left them and prayed the same prayer a third time. When He returned to His sleeping disciples, He said,

"The hour has come. Look, the Son of Man is betrayed into the hands of sinners. Rise! Let us go! Here comes my betrayer!" (Mark 14:40–42).

Betrayal

Judas Iscariot now arrived with a large crowd, armed with torches and lanterns, swords and clubs, and accompanied by a detachment of Roman soldiers. He also brought with him representatives of the religious leadership. Jesus asked who it was they wanted. He asked knowingly, wanting to protect His disciples.

"Jesus of Nazareth," they said.

"I am he," said Jesus. As He spoke, the mob fell to the ground. Jesus then asked again who it was that they were looking for.

Again they said, "Jesus of Nazareth" (John 18:4–7).

John's Gospel records Jesus' reply: "I told you that I am he. If you are looking for me, then let these men go." According to John, "this happened so that the words he had spoken would be fulfilled: 'I have not lost one of those you gave me'" (verse 9).

Now Judas came forward to greet his Master with a kiss—the prearranged signal that Jesus was the one the Romans should capture. As he did so, Jesus said, "Judas, are you betraying the Son of Man with a kiss?" (Luke 22:48) and "Friend, do what you came for" (Matthew 26:50).

The question of why Jesus had to undergo the experience of betrayal has puzzled some. Why could He not have been simply captured without betrayal? It is, of course, one of the worst forms of emotional abuse. To be betrayed by one who is an intimate friend is an experience that many face in this life. It's commonplace. As the Savior and High Priest of His people, Jesus Christ had to suffer the things we do so that He can empathize and help us when we are in need. When we suffer betrayal, He is there, knowing exactly the circumstances, the pain and the emotional turmoil. He is there to relieve that distress. When Judas came out of the darkness to betray Jesus, it was with the symbol of a close relationship—a kiss.

Another of the disciples was outraged by what was happening. As the authorities stepped forward to arrest Jesus, Peter took a sword and slashed at one of them. He struck a man named Malchus, who was the servant of the high priest. Peter's blow cut off the man's ear. Jesus' response was to tell Peter to put the sword away. He then healed Malchus's injury. "All who draw the sword will die by the sword," said Jesus (Matthew 26:52). He added that, if it were necessary, God could send a legion of angels to take care of Him. But if that happened, then He would not be able to fulfill the purpose for which He had come.

Jesus also took the opportunity to remind the mob that they were coming against Him under cover of darkness with clubs and swords, yet had failed to arrest Him in the temple when He spoke freely and openly to the people. This too, He said, was a fulfillment of the prophecies about the Messiah.

And then, as Jesus had anticipated, all of His disciples ran away, leaving Him to face torture and an excruciating death alone.

Chapter Eleven

It Is Finished

For Jesus, the wheel had come full circle. Now He would be reunited as a spirit being with His Father in heaven. But He was also to return. As the disciples stared into the heavens, two angels spoke to them and gave an enduring promise.

Once the religious and military authorities had captured Jesus of Nazareth in the Garden of Gethsemane, they bound Him and brought Him first to Annas, a powerful former high priest whose son-in-law Caiaphas now held that office. Annas asked questions about Jesus' teachings and about His disciples. Jesus said that He had spoken openly and that the authorities must ask the public what He had taught. They were the witnesses.

At this, an official hit Jesus in the face, claiming that He was being insolent toward the high priest.

Jesus responded, "If I said something wrong, testify as to what is wrong. But if I spoke the truth, why did you strike me?" (John 18:23).

Next, Jesus was taken to Caiaphas's house, where the Sanhedrin, or Council, had been called together. The fact that they were not in an official meeting place suggests that this was a hastily called meeting. They were looking for false evidence so they could put the young teacher to death.

A lot of people came forward, but none gave reason enough, including those who said that Jesus had claimed He would destroy the temple and rebuild it in three days. The claim was that He said He would replace a man-made structure with one made by God. Of course, He had not said that, and even the false witnesses could not get their testimony to agree.

The high priest asked whether Jesus was going to respond to His accusers. He remained silent until Caiaphas asked Him whether He was the Christ, the Son of God, or not. Jesus said, "Yes, it is as you say. But I say to all of you: In the future you will see the Son of Man sitting at the right hand of the Mighty One and coming on the clouds of heaven" (Matthew 26:64). Jesus was simply confirming that He would return one day, and then they would know with certainty who He was.

This was too much for the high priest. He tore his garments in outrage and branded Jesus a blasphemer. Then the others proclaimed Him worthy of death, spat on Him, insulted Him, blindfolded Him, and hit Him with their fists. They asked Him to declare by divine revelation who had just struck Him if He truly was the Son of God.

In Denial

Watching from the courtyard were two of Jesus' disciples, Peter and John. When a servant girl recognized Peter as one of Jesus' followers, he immediately denied it. This was the first of three or four denials. Jesus had foretold that Peter would deny Him three times before the cock would crow (Mark 14:30), though the Gospel accounts seem to indicate the possibility of four separate denials.

When Peter went to warm himself by a fire in the courtyard, someone else recognized him. "I don't know what you're talking about," he said (Matthew 26:70). He went to the gateway of the yard, where again he was recognized as a follower of Jesus. This time he declared with an oath that he was not. A while later, some said that his Galilean accent gave him away. Another said, "Didn't I see you with him in the olive grove?" This man was a relative of the servant whose ear Peter had severed. Now Peter became angry and cursed, denying that he knew Jesus (verses 73–74; John 18:26).

At that moment a rooster began to crow, and Jesus turned and looked at Peter. His Master's words came flooding back: "Before the rooster crows, you will disown me three times." This is not necessarily a contradiction, however. Jesus' mention of (at least) three denials does not preclude a fourth.

It was an awful moment for Peter, who had professed that he would even die with Jesus. Now he could only go outside and weep bitter tears.

At daybreak the Sanhedrin formalized their decision to put Jesus to death. They again confirmed from Jesus that He was the Son of God. "You are right in saying I am," He replied (Luke 22:70).

Judas, the betrayer, was now stricken with fear and a guilty conscience. He knew that Jesus was innocent. He took the blood money back to the chief priests and the elders, but they would have nothing more to do with him. Judas's remorse was so great that he went away and hanged himself. The religious leaders took the betrayer's reward and bought a field where strangers would be buried. It became known as the Field of Blood.

Before the Roman Ruler

The trial of Jesus, which had begun in three stages before the Jewish religious authorities, now moved into another phase, also with three stages. This time He was to appear before the political authorities. Early in the morning Jesus was led away to the palace of the Roman governor, Pontius Pilate.

Because the Jews were entering the Passover season, they didn't want to make themselves ceremonially unclean by entering the house of a gentile, so they met Pilate outside. It was an enormous hypocrisy, since they were already defiled by their condemnation of an innocent man. Pilate wanted to know the accusation against Jesus. The Jewish leaders claimed that Jesus was subverting the nation by opposing the payment of taxes to Rome and by claiming to be the Messiah, a king.

Pilate's reaction was that the Jews should judge their own people. The religious leaders declined, saying that they were not at liberty to put anyone to death. This, of course, paved the way for the crucifixion.

Pilate asked Jesus whether He was the King of the Jews. He admitted that He was, but not in any conventional sense. He explained that His kingdom was not an earthly one at that time. He acknowledged, however, that the reason He had come into the world was to establish a future kingdom. He said that He came to testify to the truth. At this Pilate showed his cynicism by asking, "What is truth?" (John 18:38).

Knowing that there was nothing in the accusation worthy of death, Pilate told the chief priests and the crowd with them that Jesus was innocent. The chief priests continued their accusations, but Jesus would not answer them. His demeanor was such that Pilate was amazed at His resilience.

The religious leaders insisted that Jesus had started a campaign in Galilee and had now brought it to Jerusalem. This gave Pilate an idea. He asked Jesus if He was a Galilean. When he understood that Jesus was under Herod Antipas's jurisdiction, he sent Him to Herod, who was in Jerusalem at the time.

Herod had long wanted to meet Jesus. He hoped to see a miracle performed. He had, of course, murdered John the Baptist and refused to repent of his adulterous union with his brother's wife. But Herod's interest in Jesus was nothing more than curiosity. That became clear when Jesus would not answer his questions. So Herod and his soldiers mocked

Him and sent Him back to Pilate, dressed in a kingly robe. It proved to be a perfect opportunity for Herod and Pilate to become friends—they had been enemies until this incident with Jesus (Luke 23:6–12).

It was an annual custom for the Roman ruler to release a prisoner chosen by the crowds. Pilate had already tried a couple of ways to free Jesus and failed. Now he tried a third. There was a man in prison, a murderer named Barabbas, who had led a rebellion. Pilate offered the crowds the choice between Jesus and this man. He must have believed that they would not choose a murderer over a man whom both he and Herod had found innocent. Pilate knew that Jesus was the victim of religious envy. Yet the crowd was incited to demand the release of Barabbas (verses 13–19; Matthew 27:15–18).

At that very moment Pilate's wife sent him a message. She said that she had had a troubling dream about Jesus and implored her husband to have nothing to do with the innocent man (Matthew 27:19). But the crowd continued to demand the release of Barabbas. Pilate now felt that he had no choice, so he sent Jesus to be flogged. The Roman soldiers plaited a thorny crown and put it on Jesus' head. They dressed Him in a purple robe, hit Him in the face, and mocked and abused Him.

Again Pilate went to the crowd to protest Jesus' innocence. Again he asked what should be done with Him. The crowd roared for His crucifixion. Pilate nevertheless persisted in trying to release Jesus: "Why?" he asked. "What crime has this man committed? I have found in him no grounds for the death penalty. Therefore I will have him punished and then release him" (Luke 23:22). But the cry for crucifixion went up again.

Pilate told the Jewish leaders, "You take him and crucify him." He even went back to Jesus to plead with Him for a way out. He asked, "Don't you realize I have power either to free you or to crucify you?" (John 19:6b–10). Jesus explained to him that he had no power that had not been granted by God.

Again Pilate tried to release Jesus, but to no avail. Now the Roman governor took a bowl of water and washed his hands in front of the crowd to symbolize that he would not be held to account for the death of an innocent man. The crowd willingly took on the responsibility.

Pilate released Barabbas, had Jesus flogged, and handed Him over to be crucified. The Roman soldiers took another opportunity to mock and beat Him as He was dressed again in a purple robe. Then they gave Him back his own clothes and led Him out to a place on the edge of the city, called Golgotha, which means "the place of a skull." Along the way, a man from Cyrene in North Africa was forced to carry what was probably the crossbeam of Jesus' crucifixion stake. Jesus had carried it but was now too weak to go on.

When they led Jesus to the place of His death, He was accompanied by two criminals who were also to be executed.

Jesus on the Stake

The crucifixion of Jesus Christ is probably one of the most enduring images in Western culture. It has been a continuous subject of art and literature for 2,000 years. Perhaps in the resulting fictionalization it has lost its power and a great deal of its significance for people.

What exactly do the Gospels tell us about it?

Matthew's Gospel begins the account with a simple recognition that the act of crucifixion had occurred. He writes, "When they had crucified him, they divided up his clothes by casting lots" (Matthew 27:35).

Matthew does not mean that Jesus was dead. He is saying that the nailing of the victim to the cross, or stake, had been carried out, and the condemned was left to die an agonizing death. The four soldiers who were guarding the three men hanging before them were now busy sharing the spoils; all that was left were the clothes of the victims. In Jesus' case they shared what they could, but His undergarment was seamless. So they cast lots for it rather than tear it apart.

Jesus knew that the soldiers had little understanding of what they were doing in crucifying Him. His attitude toward them was not born of malice. He simply said, "Father, forgive them, for they do not know what they are doing" (Luke 23:34). This was the first of seven statements that Jesus made during His crucifixion. All of this began to happen at about nine o'clock in the morning.

Over Jesus' head, Pilate had ordered that a sign be placed, which read in Aramaic, Latin and Greek, "This is Jesus of Nazareth, the King of the Jews." The chief priests had objected to Pilate's wording, but Pilate responded, "What I have written, I have written" (John 19:22).

Many people from Jerusalem were able to read what the sign said as they passed by. A number of them shouted insults at Jesus. The elders and the teachers of the law mocked Him, saying that if He really were the Son of God He would save Himself. The soldiers and even the two robbers crucified with Him began to taunt Him.

One of the two seemed to make worse accusations than the other. The second one was afraid that God would punish them further for insulting an innocent man. He said, "We deserve our punishment, but this man has done nothing wrong" (Luke 23:41, paraphrased). He asked Jesus to remember him when the kingdom of God would come. Jesus assured him that the day would come when the robber would be with Him in His kingdom, referred to here as "paradise."

Standing near the crucifixion was Jesus' mother, Mary. From the time of His conception she had thought deeply about the unique son she was to raise. Now she stood at the foot of His execution stake. Jesus saw her there with a number of other women, including Mary Magdalene. The disciple John was also standing nearby and watching. Jesus told His mother that she would now have John as a son, and to John He said that he would have a new mother. From then on John took care of Mary.

Death of the Innocent

At noon an unusual darkness fell over the land. It was to last for the next three hours, during which Jesus came to the point of death. At about three o'clock in the afternoon He shouted in a loud voice, "My God, my God, why have you forsaken me?" (Matthew 27:46; Mark 15:34). It was the awful, agonized cry of a human being cut off and separated from God, bearing the penalty for human sin. Jesus was guilty of nothing sinful. He died as an innocent sacrifice in place of every human who has lived, who lives now, or who will live. The death of the Son of God in our stead means that His life was given for ours. We can therefore be forgiven and avoid suffering the death penalty for sin. The enormity of what Jesus was willing to go through so that we could be forgiven and ultimately live forever is often obscured by the fictionalizing of the reality of His crucifixion.

Knowing that the end was near, Jesus said, "I am thirsty" (John 19:28). They gave Him wine vinegar on a sponge at the end of a hyssop stalk. At last He could say, "It is finished" (verse 30). Then with another loud cry He called out, "Father, into your hands I commit my spirit" (Luke 23:46). With this the Savior of humanity bowed His head and breathed His last breath.

At the moment of Jesus' death, miraculous events took place in and around Jerusalem. In the temple, the curtain that separated the Holy of Holies was torn in two from top to bottom. An earthquake opened the tombs of some of the people of God, and they were brought back to physical life.

The soldiers guarding Jesus were terrified at the earthquake and all that was happening. The centurion, who heard Jesus' final cry and saw how He died, said, "Surely he was the Son of God" (Matthew 27:51–54).

Those followers of Jesus who were present stood at a distance to see what would happen next. Among them were many women, including Mary Magdalene; Mary, the mother of James and Joses; and Salome. When Jesus was teaching in Galilee, these were some of the women who took care of Him.

The day of Jesus' death, a Wednesday, was a time of preparation for the first holy day of the Feast of Unleavened Bread (Mark 15:42; John 19:31; see also Leviticus 23:4–8). The religious leaders did not want the three condemned men hanging on crucifixes on the holy day, referred to in John's Gospel as "a special Sabbath." They went to Pilate, the Roman governor, and asked that the legs of the victims be broken so that they would die more quickly. Unable to support their own weight, the crucified men would soon suffocate. The soldiers came and broke the legs of the two robbers, but when they saw that Jesus was already dead, they left Him alone. The fact is that earlier, while Jesus was still alive, one of the soldiers had rammed a spear into His side, causing a rush of blood and water. Jesus had died from that sudden loss of blood. John records that he himself saw these things and that he is telling the truth (John 19:31–35).

As evening approached, a wealthy man—Joseph of Arimathea, a member of the Jewish Council and a follower of Jesus—came to Pilate and asked for Jesus' body. Of course, Joseph had not been party to the Council's plot against his Teacher. Pilate was surprised that Jesus was already dead and asked the centurion whether it was true. When it was confirmed, Pilate gave the body to Joseph, who took it and placed it in his own new tomb in a garden nearby Golgotha.

Another man, Nicodemus, who was also a member of the Sanhedrin and had visited Jesus by night early in His ministry, joined Joseph. Together they prepared Jesus' body for immediate burial with myrrh and aloes and wrapped it with strips of linen. Then they rolled a stone across the entrance to the tomb.

Not on a Sunday

All of this had been watched by some of the women from Galilee. As the evening came they went home, because it was the beginning of the high holy day (verses 38–42; Luke 23:50–56).

On the holy day, which was a Thursday, the chief priests and Pharisees went to Pilate and requested that a guard be placed at the tomb so that no one could steal Jesus' body. They said that Jesus had claimed He would be resurrected after three days. Pilate granted their request. The religious leaders set the soldiers at the site and put a seal on the large stone covering the tomb.

Luke records that the women from Galilee prepared spices and perfumes for further treatment of the body. They would not have done so on the holy day, so they must have done it on Friday (Mark 16:1). Luke tells us that they rested on the Sabbath according to the command (Luke 23:56). That would have been Saturday.

Luke continues the account by saying that "on the first day of the week, very early in the morning, the women took the spices they had prepared and went to the tomb" (Luke 24:1). What did they find there? When they arrived, to their surprise the large stone covering the entrance to the tomb was already rolled out of the way and Jesus' body was nowhere to be seen. Then two angelic beings appeared and explained that Jesus had risen from the dead and that He was going ahead to Galilee. The women were told to go and tell this to the disciples. All of this occurred on Sunday morning.

But the reality is that counting forward three days and three nights from Wednesday afternoon or early evening brings us to late Saturday afternoon or early evening. Jesus' resurrection took place not at the traditionally accepted time of Sunday morning but hours earlier.

At the time He was resurrected there was another earthquake, and an angel rolled back the stone from the tomb's entrance. He then sat on the stone, and the sight of him terrified the guards so that they ran away. The women did not discover Jesus' resurrection until Sunday, very early in the morning, at which time the angels told them, "He has risen" (verse 6).

This has been a source of confusion for a long time. There have been those who have known that the resurrection was not on Sunday, but when you come up against tradition, it is often almost impossible to dislodge false ideas from the mind.

The Resurrection Is Real

When the women returned and told the disciples what had happened, the men thought they were talking nonsense. But Peter and John ran to the tomb to check their story. John, arriving first, looked in and saw the linen grave wrappings lying there. He wondered what it could mean. When Peter arrived, he went into the tomb and saw the strips of linen and the cloth that had been wrapped around the head of the dead body neatly folded nearby. John records that he went inside himself and was then convinced that Jesus was alive. But he also says that the disciples did not yet understand from Scripture that Jesus would be resurrected.

Perhaps this is why they returned home, leaving Mary Magdalene weeping at the tomb. When she looked into the sepulcher, she saw two angels sitting at the head and foot of the place where Jesus' body had lain. They asked her why she was crying. She replied that Jesus had been taken away and she did not know where His body was. Then she turned around and saw a man. He, too, asked why she was crying and for whom she was looking. Thinking he was a gardener, she said, "Sir, if you have carried him away, tell me where you have put him, and I will get him" (John 20:1–15).

It was, of course, Jesus. He said simply, "Mary." She turned and said in recognition, "Rabboni!" which means "My Teacher" in Aramaic. Jesus told her not to hold on to Him, saying that He had not yet returned to His Father. He said that she must go back to the disciples and tell them that He said, "I am returning to my Father and your Father, to my God and your God" (verses 16–17).

This was one of at least 10 post-resurrection appearances that Jesus was to make over the next several weeks. Another was to the other women who had been at the tomb. Jesus came to them after they had left the empty sepulcher. He told them to tell the disciples that they should go to Galilee, where He would meet them.

At this point in the narrative we read that some of the guards who had been frightened away from the tomb went to the chief priests and told them what had happened. The religious authorities decided to concoct a story to offset what would happen when people heard that Jesus' body had disappeared. They paid the soldiers a large sum to say that the disciples had stolen the body. This, they said, would calm the governor, Pontius Pilate, if he found out that Jesus' body was no longer in the tomb (Matthew 28:11–14). The story was widely circulated and became the account that many people believed.

One Man's Doubts

Toward the end of that first day of the week, after His resurrection, Jesus also appeared to two disciples who were returning to Emmaus, seven miles outside Jerusalem. They were prevented from recognizing Jesus as He walked alongside them on the road. He asked what they were discussing. They were obviously depressed. One of the two, Cleopas, asked whether the stranger had been in Jerusalem in the past few days. Surely he knew what had happened to Jesus of Nazareth.

They mentioned how the authorities had put Him to death, but that now His tomb was found empty and reports had come back that He had been resurrected.

Jesus said to them, "How foolish you are, and how slow of heart to believe all that the prophets have spoken! Did not the Christ have to suffer these things and then enter his glory?" From there He opened their minds to understand all that had been written about Him by Moses and the prophets. He showed that His life, death and resurrection had fulfilled many of the prophecies (Luke 24:13–27).

When they arrived at the village, Jesus made as if He were going on farther. They insisted that He stay with them, because it was getting dark. That evening they sat down for a meal together. It was only when He took bread, gave thanks and broke it and gave it to them that they recognized Him. He then disappeared. They agreed that they had sensed something unusual as He talked with them on the road, but they hadn't known what it was.

As a result of this experience they returned to Jerusalem immediately and found the disciples excitedly saying that Jesus was alive and had appeared to Peter. The two disciples from Emmaus then recounted what had happened to them.

At this point Jesus Himself appeared in the midst of them. They were all terrified, thinking they had seen a ghost. He told them not to be troubled, that He was real, that He had flesh and bones.

He invited them to examine the wounds in His hands, feet and side. Then He shared some food with them, demonstrating that He was not a ghost. He told them again that they would receive the Holy Spirit to help them in carrying out the work ahead.

Thomas was a doubtful disciple. He was not present when Jesus came among them, so when the others told him what they had seen, he said that he would not believe unless Jesus met some stringent tests. Thomas wanted to see the crucifixion nail prints in His hands and the wound in His side before he would believe that Jesus was alive (John 20:24–25).

A week later Jesus appeared among the disciples again. This time Thomas was there. Now Jesus invited Thomas to free himself of his doubts by doing exactly what he had demanded. He put his finger into the nail holes and reached his hand into Jesus' wounded side. Now he was convinced, but Jesus said those who believed without such direct evidence would be blessed. Nevertheless, as a result of what he saw, Thomas gave the strongest confirmation of Jesus' identity. He said, "My Lord and my God!" (verse 28). It was the first time anyone had made such a confession, naming Jesus as God.

John mentions that Jesus did many other miraculous signs in the presence of His disciples, but that many are not recorded. The few that are set down, he writes, should be proof enough that Jesus is the Son of God, the Messiah, through whom eternal life becomes possible (verses 30–31).

More Evidence

The next two appearances Jesus made were in Galilee. First He came to seven of the disciples as they were fishing. They had worked all night and caught nothing. Now, early in the morning, a figure stood on the shore and asked whether they had netted anything. They had to say no. He then told them to cast to the right. When they did, they caught so many fish that they couldn't haul in the net. It was reminiscent of the time He had performed a similar miracle and then called some of them to be His disciples (John 21:1–6; see also Luke 5:1–11).

John was the first to recognize the stranger standing at the side of the lake. He said, "It is the Lord!" (John 21:7). As soon as Peter heard it, he jumped into the water. By the time the others reached the shore about a hundred yards away, they saw a fire burning, with fish and bread ready to eat. Jesus asked them to bring some more fish to cook.

When they had finished their meal, Jesus asked Peter three times whether he loved Him more than his other companions. Peter reassured Jesus that he did. But Jesus was anxious to coax out of Peter a genuine commitment to care for the people of God. He warned him that he, too, would die an ignominious death. Then He said to Peter, "Follow me" (verses 15–19).

Peter was curious as to what would happen to John in the future. Jesus replied that it was not for Peter to know. John ends his Gospel at this point in the history of Christ's life by assuring us that many other things could have been written about Him, but that these are the necessary facts.

Jesus is recorded as having appeared four more times to His followers. One was at a mountain location in Galilee where the 11 were present. Some of them were still doubtful. Here Jesus gave them a commission to go into the world and teach those God would call to obey the things that He,

Christ, had commanded. He promised that He would be with His people through the end of this present age of man (Matthew 28:16–20).

On another occasion He appeared to 500 disciples at the same time. When the apostle Paul recorded this, perhaps 20 years later, he said that most of the people who had seen Him were still alive. Jesus also appeared to His own half brother James, who later became leader of the Jerusalem church (1 Corinthians 15:6–7).

The Promise of Return

Over the course of several weeks following His resurrection, Jesus' disciples saw Him many times. He instructed them to stay in Jerusalem until the Holy Spirit came (Acts 1:3–5). That occurred very soon afterward, on Pentecost.

His final appearance to the disciples took place just before He left them to return to the Father. He explained that they would be witnesses to all that had happened during the three and a half years they had been together with Him. Some wanted to know whether He would immediately set up the kingdom of God on the earth. He told them that the Father would bring that about according to His own time frame, not theirs (verses 6–8).

At the end of 40 days, while they were all together on the Mount of Olives, He was taken up from them and disappeared from sight into a cloud. For Jesus, the wheel had come full circle. Now He would be reunited as a spirit being with His Father in heaven. But He was also to return. As the disciples stared into the heavens, two angels spoke to them and gave an enduring promise. They said, in appropriate conclusion to the account of Jesus' life as a human being: "Men of Galilee, why do you stand here looking into the sky? This same Jesus, who has been taken from you into heaven, will come back in the same way you have seen him go into heaven" (verses 9–11).

This was the very promise that Jesus Himself had given weeks earlier on the same Mount of Olives, when He had explained to His disciples the prophetic sequence that would precede His return (see Matthew 24:3, 30). The four separate Gospel accounts end with Christ's commissioning the disciples to go out into the world carrying His message of the coming kingdom of God; with His return to His Father; and with His promised second coming.

Despite the intervening 20 centuries since the life of Jesus of Nazareth and the events the Gospels describe, the accounts have as much if not more relevance to our age, because we need the truths they impart in order to live successfully in a far more complex world. The accounts of the life and teachings of Jesus Christ continue to reach out with profound relevance to us, who desperately need the Gospels for the 21st century.